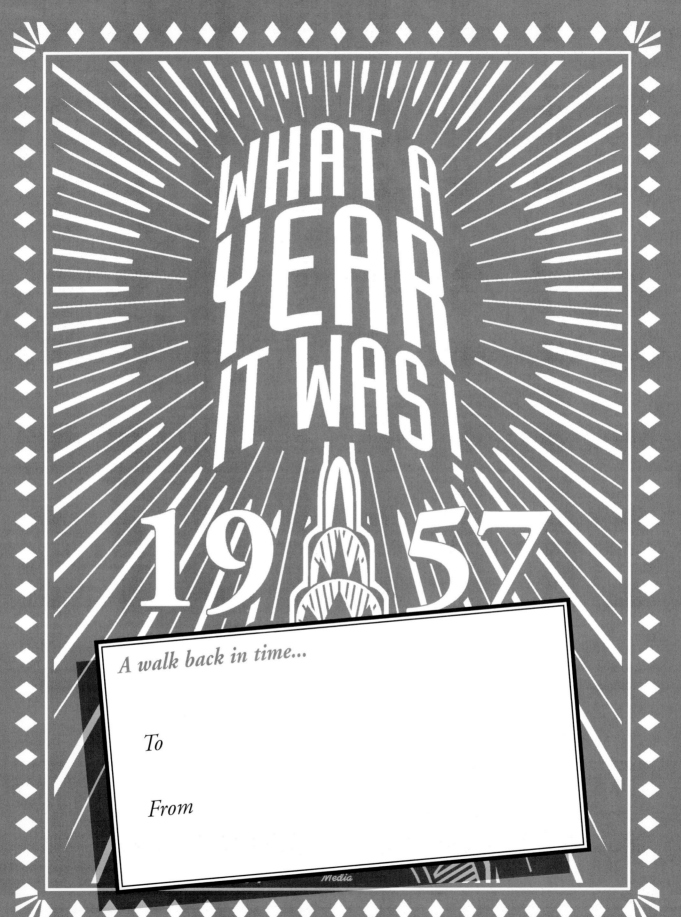

WHAT A YEAR IT WAS!

1957

A walk back in time...

To

From

*Dedicated to America's men and women*
*who risked and lost their lives*
*in the Korean War.*

*Publishers* • Lawrence Siegel & Arthur Worthington
*Designers* • Peter Hess & Marguerite Jones
*Writing & Research* • Beverly Cohn & Peter Hess
*Facilitator* • Pamela Thomas

## www.FLICKBACK.com
(800) 541-3533

# *Contents*

Arts
&
Entertainment

A number of foreign directors have big years with award-winning films. Italian **Federico Fellini**'s *Nights of Cabiria*, concerning a charming prostitute, is an international hit. Swedish director **Ingmar Bergman**'s serious cinematic inquiries into the nature of life and death, *The Seventh Seal* and *Wild Strawberries*, receive worldwide critical acclaim. **Satyajit Ray**, from India, completes *Aparajito*, the second in his trilogy about the appealing boy, Apu. *Throne of Blood* is Japanese director **Akira Kurosawa**'s re-staging of *Macbeth* as a Samurai epic.

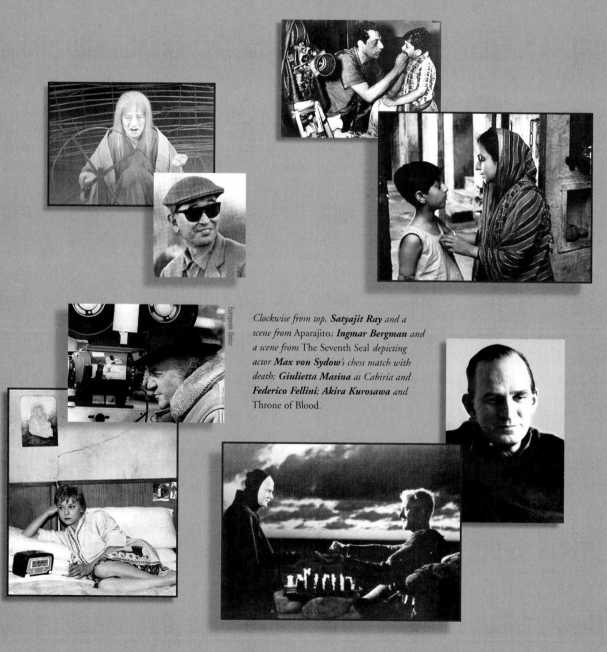

European Union

*Clockwise from top,* **Satyajit Ray** *and a scene from* Aparajito; **Ingmar Bergman** *and a scene from* The Seventh Seal *depicting actor* **Max von Sydow**'s *chess match with death;* **Giulietta Masina** *as Cabiria and* **Federico Fellini**; **Akira Kurosawa** *and* Throne of Blood.

# Movies

## DRIVE-IN NIGHTS

For many Americans, the movie-going experience means parking under the stars in drive-in theaters, which number around 4,000 nationwide. In the privacy and relative anonymity of their cars, audiences indulge their taste for "shocking" juvenile delinquent and girls-gone-bad double features. Teasing advertisements featuring shapely women and black leather jacket-clad rumblers often promise more thrills than the low-budget potboilers can deliver. Among the titles packing them in: *The Delinquents, The Girl in Black Stockings, Hot Rod Rumble* ("The slick chicks who fire up the big wheels!"), *Motorcycle Gang, Naked Paradise, Reform School Girl, Rock All Night* (Some have to dance... some have to kill!) and *Young and Dangerous*. Even comic **Jerry Lewis** gets a piece of the action as a shaky bad boy in *The Delicate Delinquent*.

# at the
# MOVIES

Marilyn Monroe picture that teases and tickles like

**Marilyn Monroe** starring with
**Laurence Olivier** in Warner Bros
**The Prince and the Showgirl**

Some countries have a medal for Everything.

LIFE IS IN THEIR HANDS— DEATH IS ON THEIR MINDS!

IT **EXPLODES** LIKE 12 STICKS OF DYNAMITE!

**HENRY FONDA**
# 12 ANGRY MEN

with LEE J. COBB · ED BEGLEY and E. G. MARSHALL · JACK WARDEN · Story and Screenplay by REGINALD ROSE
Directed by SIDNEY LUMET · Produced by HENRY FONDA and REGINALD ROSE
An ORION-NOVA Production · Released thru UNITED ARTISTS · Associate Producer GEORGE JUSTIN

"A MAGNIFICENT, MOVING FILM!"
LIFE Magazine

"DESTINED TO BECOME A CLASSIC!"
LOOK Magazine

HECHT-HILL and LANCASTER present
**BURT LANCASTER**
**TONY CURTIS**
in
*Sweet Smell of Success*

The Motion Picture That Will Never Be Forgiven— Or Forgotten!

**MARLON BRANDO**

TECHNIRAMA
TECHNICOLOR
REGIA DI
JOSHUA LOGAN

# SAYONARA

COLUMBIA PICTURES
presents
A SAM SPIEGEL PRODUCTION

**WILLIAM HOLDEN**
**ALEC GUINNESS · JACK HAWK**
in
# "THE BRIDGE ON THE RIVER KWAI"
CINEMASCOPE    TECHNICOLOR

with SESSUE HAYAKAWA · JAMES DONALD · ANN SEARS and introducing GEOFFREY HORNE
Directed by DAVID LEAN · Screenplay by PIERRE BOULLE Based on His Novel

20th CENTURY-FOX presents
# CARY GRANT
# DEBORAH KERR

in
Leo McCarey's AN AFFAIR TO REMEMBER

COLOR by DE LUXE
CINEMASCOPE

RICHARD DENNING · NEVA PATTERSON · CATHLEEN NESBITT · ROBERT Q. LEWIS · CHARLES WATTS · FORTUNATO BONANOVA
PRODUCED BY JERRY WALD · LEO McCAREY · DELMER DAVES and LEO McCAREY

AUDREY
# HEPBURN
FRED ASTAIRE

# FUNNY FACE
KAY THOMPSON

with MICHEL AUCLAIR · ROBERT FLEMYNG
MUSIC and LYRICS by GEORGE and IRA GERSHWIN

All the heart, all the excitement of a great frontier adventure!

# WALT DISNEY
presents
DOROTHY McGUIRE and FESS PARKER

# OLD YELLER
TECHNICOLOR

An Affair To Remember
The Bridge On The River Kwai
Desk Set
Edge Of The City
Enemy Below
A Face In The Crowd
Funny Face
Gunfight At The O.K. Corral
A Hatful Of Rain
Heaven Knows, Mr. Allison
Island In The Sun
The James Dean Story
A King In New York
Les Girls
Love In The Afternoon
Man Of A Thousand Faces
Man On Fire
Old Yeller
The Pajama Game
Pal Joey
Paths Of Glory
Peyton Place
The Prince And The Showgirl
Raintree County
Saint Joan
Sayonara
Silk Stockings
The Spirit Of St. Louis
The Sun Also Rises
The Sweet Smell Of Success
Tammy And The Bachelor
This Could Be The Night
Three Faces Of Eve
Twelve Angry Men
Witness For The Prosecution

1957

*an
abundant
year for*

HORROR
&
SCI-FI

9

# TOP STARS
## of '57

Rock **Hudson**
John **Wayne**
Sophia **Loren**
Marilyn **Monroe**
Frank **Sinatra**
Gary **Cooper**
William **Holden**
James **Stewart**
Jerry **Lewis**
Yul **Brynner**

# NEW STARS
## of '57

Carroll **Baker**
Pat **Boone**
Anita **Ekberg**
Martha **Hyer**
John **Kerr**
Jayne **Mansfield**
Don **Murray**
Paul **Newman**
Anthony **Perkins**
Elvis **Presley**

*John Wayne*

*Marilyn Monroe*

*Paul Newman*

*Carroll Baker*

**Elvis Presley**'s second film, *Loving You*, is released, quickly followed by *Jailhouse Rock*, which spawns the #1 hit record of the same name.

10

# The Academy Awards

"And The Winner Is..."

## Oscars® Presented in 1957

**BEST PICTURE**
*AROUND THE WORLD IN 80 DAYS*

**BEST ACTOR**
YUL BRYNNER,
*The King And I*

**BEST ACTRESS**
INGRID BERGMAN,
*Anastasia*

**BEST DIRECTOR**
GEORGE STEVENS, *Giant*

**BEST SUPPORTING ACTOR**
ANTHONY QUINN, *Lust for Life*

**BEST SUPPORTING ACTRESS**
DOROTHY MALONE, *Written On The Wind*

**BEST SONG**
"WHATEVER WILL BE, WILL BE (QUE SERA, SERA),"
*The Man Who Knew Too Much*

*Yul Brynner*

## 1957 Favorites (Oscars® Presented in 1958)

**BEST PICTURE**
*THE BRIDGE ON THE RIVER KWAI*

**BEST ACTOR**
ALEC GUINNESS,
*The Bridge On The River Kwai*

**BEST ACTRESS**
JOANNE WOODWARD,
*The Three Faces Of Eve*

**BEST DIRECTOR**
DAVID LEAN,
*The Bridge On The River Kwai*

**BEST SUPPORTING ACTOR**
RED BUTTONS, *Sayonara*

**BEST SUPPORTING ACTRESS**
MIYOSHI UMEKI, *Sayonara*

**BEST SONG**
"ALL THE WAY," *The Joker Is Wild*

*Miyoshi Umeki*

**F**ans gather outside the Pantages Theatre in Hollywood to watch their favorite movie stars arrive for the

# 29th Annual Academy Awards.

**A** special ovation greets **Janet Gaynor**, who was the first to receive the Best Actress award in 1928.

**B**eaming **Robert Stack** is nominated as Best Supporting Actor for his performance in *Written On The Wind*.

**A**nthony **Quinn** receives his second Oscar nomination for his performance in *Lust For Life*.

**J**ack Lemmon presents the Best Supporting Actress award to **Dorothy Malone** for her role in *Written On The Wind*.

**A**n overjoyed Miss Malone makes her acceptance speech.

**I**n **Ingrid Bergman**'s absence, **Cary Grant** accepts the Best Actress award for her performance in *Anastasia*.

**Y**ul Brynner receives his Oscar from **Anna Magnani** for the Best Actor for his performance in *The King And I*.

**Mitzi Gaynor** presents the Best Picture award to director **Mike Todd** for his production, *Around The World In 80 Days*.

**Dorothy Malone** and **Anthony Quinn** show off their awards.

# Memorable Lines

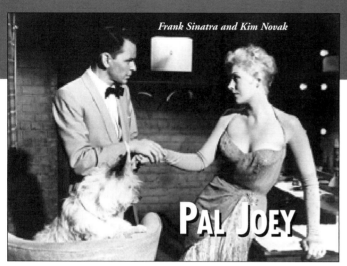
*Frank Sinatra and Kim Novak*

## PAL JOEY

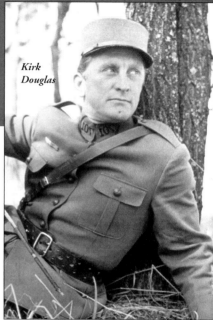
*Kirk Douglas*

## PATHS OF GLORY

Linda English: *Why do people drink when you feel so awful the morning after?*
Joey Evans: *Maybe because it feels so good the night before.*

Linda English: *What did I do last night?*
Joey Evans: *You kissed me.*
Linda English: *I wasn't myself.*
Joey Evans: *Whoever you were, you were great!*

General Broulard: ***Colonel Dax! You will apologize at once or I shall have you placed under arrest!***
Colonel Dax: *I apologize... for not being entirely honest with you. I apologize for not revealing my true feelings. I apologize, sir, for not telling you sooner that you're a degenerate, sadistic old man. And you can go to hell before I apologize to you now or ever again!*

## WITNESS FOR THE PROSECUTION

*Charles Laughton and Marlene Dietrich*

Leonard Vole: *But this is England, where I thought you never arrest, let alone convict, people for crimes they have not committed.*

Sir Wilfrid: *We try not to make a habit of it.*

Sir Wilfrid: *I am constantly surprised that women's hats do not provoke more murders.*

*Tony Curtis and Burt Lancaster*

## Sweet Smell of Success

Sam: *But Sidney, you make a living. Where do you want to get?*
Sidney Falco: *Way up high, Sam, where it's always balmy. Where no one snaps his fingers and says, "Hey, Shrimp, rack the balls!" or, "Hey, mouse, mouse, go out and buy me a pack of butts." I don't want tips from the kitty. I'm in the big game with the big players... In brief, from now on, the best of everything is good enough for me.*

J.J. Hunsecker: *You're dead, son. Get yourself buried.*

# Celebrities Attend The Premiere In New York Of "The Great Man" Starring Jose Ferrer

WORLD PREMIERE TUESDAY JANUARY IST
JOSE FERRER ~ "THE GREAT MAN"

Opera star ROBERT MERRILL and his wife attend the premiere.

A smiling SAMMY DAVIS, JR. attends festivities alone.

AL MORGAN, author of the best selling novel on which the movie is based, attends the premiere with VICKY DUGAN.

Pals ROBERT ALDA (right), STUBBY KAYE (center) and BILLY GOLDBERG attend this festive event.

# *BATTLE HYMN* Premieres In Korean War Hero Colonel Dean Hess' Hometown With Two Days Of Festivities

**M**arietta, Ohio stages the greatest civic celebration in its history to welcome **Colonel Dean Hess** and the premiere of his dramatic film biography, *Battle Hymn*.

**A** lavish banquet is given honoring the Colonel.

**F**estivities continue for two days including this parade honoring all those associated with the film.

**R**ock Hudson, who plays the Colonel in the film, makes his way through a most enthusiastic crowd.

**R**ock Hudson, pictured with **Dan Duryea**.

16

The parson who became an ace airman saved thousands of Korean orphans from capture by the reds.

Celebrating Founder's Day, Marietta College bestows an honorary degree on Rock Hudson.

The festivities culminate with the premiere and the biggest crowd ever gathering outside the theatre.

Rock Hudson, Colonel Hess and a City Father smile at the crowd as they get ready to enter the theatre.

# Now you can run your color-slide show from anywhere in the room!

## NEW ARGUS REMOTE CONTROL SLIDE PROJECTOR

ONLY $ **85.00**   Most dealers offer budget terms . . . as little as $8.50 down.

Just relax in your favorite easy chair or sofa . . . anywhere in the room . . . while you run a really professional color-slide show with this great new Argus Remote Control Projector.

You just press the button on the compact, hand-fitting control switch to *automatically* show, change and return your slides to their proper places in the magazine. And you can change from remote to direct control any time you wish.

This finest of all Argus projectors also offers you all these other precision features: an exclusive new light condenser system — to give you brighter, clearer pictures; a new wide-angle lens — to give you big, life-size pictures even in a small room.

In addition, there's a compact, 36-slide aluminum magazine—to protect slides from dirt and dog-earing; a powerful blower—to keep slides and projector cool during long showings; a handy Slide Editor—to let you preview slides and arrange them in story-telling sequence.

Stop in at your Argus dealer's soon. Let him show you how beautiful color slides can be . . . and how easily and inexpensively you can show them . . . with this new Argus Remote Control Projector.

Complete with carrying case, slide magazine and 15 ft. of control cord.

Color slides cost surprisingly little . . . only 5 cents more than ordinary black-and-white prints—just about a third as much as color prints! You see your slides big as life on a screen, and when you're not showing them, they're stored in compact aluminum magazines.

Argus projector prices start at $39.50. All Argus projectors, including the $39.50 Argus 300 (shown at right), have an exclusive optical system that gives you bigger pictures even in a small room. The Argus Automatic Projector—without remote control is priced at only $62.50.

# argus ®

*Argus Cameras, Ann Arbor, Michigan.*
*Division of Sylvania Electric Products Inc.*

**WORLD'S NO. 1 NAME IN COLOR-SLIDE PHOTOGRAPHY**

*Michelle Pfeiffer*

**BORN IN 1957** ★
**LEVAR BURTON** ★
**STEVE BUSCEMI** ★
**GEENA DAVIS** ★
**STEPHEN FRY** ★
**MELANIE GRIFFITH** ★ **SPIKE LEE**
★ **DANIEL-DAY LEWIS** ★ **KELLY
McGILLIS** ★ **MICHELLE PFEIFFER** ★
**THERESA RUSSELL** ★ **JULIAN
SANDS** ★ **ROBERT
TOWNSEND** ★
**MARIO VAN PEEBLES**
★ **RACHEL WARD**

*Daniel-Day Lewis*

☆ **Rita Hayworth** fulfills her 20-year contract with Columbia Pictures, returning to the screen after a three-year absence.

☆ *Island In The Sun* starring **James Mason**, **Dorothy Dandridge**, **Joan Fontaine** and **Harry Belafonte** is the first film to depict an interracial romance.

☆ Well-scrubbed singer **Pat Boone** makes his screen debut with **Shirley Jones** in *April Love*.

☆ 50% of the nation's teenagers see at least one movie a week.

☆ 1,200 movie theaters close as audiences turn to other sources of entertainment, including television.

☆ Hanna-Barbera Productions is created when "Tom & Jerry" animators **Joseph Barbera** and **William Hanna** join forces.

## HOLLYWOOD BIDS A FOND FAREWELL

Iconic actor **Humphrey Bogart** dies at 57, leaving an unmatched body of film work including HIGH SIERRA, THE MALTESE FALCON, CASABLANCA, THE CAINE MUTINY and his Academy Award winning performance in THE AFRICAN QUEEN.

**Oliver Hardy**, half of the greatest comedy team in the history of movies, dies at age 65.

*Oliver Hardy, right, with Stan Laurel*

**Louis B. Mayer**, co-founder of MGM and architect of Hollywood's star system, dies at 72.

Director/actor **Erich von Stroheim** is dead at age 71.

Silent screen star **Norma Talmadge** dies at 60.

*Humphrey Bogart*

So simple to tune—even a child can do it. The *Aldrich* (above) in limed oak grained finish (21CS781). $495.

**21" PICTURE TUBE***
*OVERALL DIAMETER—254 SQUARE INCHES OF VIEWABLE PICTURE

**Big as life.** Even the lowest priced RCA Victor Big Color set gives a huge 254 square inches of viewable picture—crisp and clear in black-and-white or Color.

**All the colors of life.** RCA Victor Big Color TV gives Color so natural, so alive—you have to see it to believe it. It's a completely new experience in home entertainment.

**Practical and dependable.** Big Color TV service is low-cost—RCA Victor Factory Service Contracts available in most areas, but only to owners of RCA Victor TV.

**Like 2 sets in 1** because it's RCA Victor *Compatible* Color. Color shows in Color—all others in black-and-white. This is today's common-sense investment in TV.

# "LIVING COLOR" AT $495 IS NOW BEST TV BUY–IT'S LIKE 2 SETS IN 1

**See Color every night — see black-and-white shows, too. RCA Victor Big Color is today's best TV investment!**

**Here is double-value** Color TV at the lowest price in RCA Victor history. Now you and your family will see every program *exactly* as it is broadcast. . . . big Color shows in breath-taking "Living Color"—all regular programs in crisp, clear black-and-white.

**New "Color-Quick" tuning**—simple, fast, accurate. Turn two knobs and the screen blossoms out in Color. Even a child can tune it.

**Your choice of 10 Big Color models**—from table model to full-door console in contemporary or traditional styling.

**See "Living Color"** with your own eyes at your RCA Victor dealer's soon. Ask him about easy budget terms on any Big Color set—your present TV may even cover the down payment!

Manufacturer's nationally advertised VHF list price shown. UHF optional, extra. Prices and specifications subject to change. **At your service:** RCA Victor Factory Service Contracts from $39.95 (90 days).

**RCA VICTOR**
RADIO CORPORATION OF AMERICA
RCA PIONEERED AND DEVELOPED COMPATIBLE COLOR TV

# Television

## MUSICAL CHAIRS

Busy **Steve Allen**, the original host of *The Tonight Show* since its 1954 debut, departs the program in January to concentrate on other projects, including his own Sunday night show opposite **Ed Sullivan**. **Ernie Kovacs**, who handles *Tonight's* hosting duties Monday and Tuesday nights, leaves as

*Steve Allen*

well. NBC decides to try a version of *Tonight* modeled on its popular morning *Today Show*. The new chatty news format *Tonight! America After Dark*, hosted by **Jack Lescoulie**, quickly proves unsuccessful and is

replaced mid-year by *Tonight starring Jack Paar*, with the new popular host reverting to the original talk show format.

Meanwhile, after spending almost all of his 4 1/2 years with **Dave Garroway** on the *Today Show*, mascot **J. Fred Muggs**, the world's most successful chimpanzee, quits to seek greener trees. Having amassed a fortune between salary and product endorsements, the wealthy Mr. Muggs is the envy of a lot of show biz folks.

- ■ *Maverick* and *Have Gun Will Travel* are among 10 new Westerns making their TV debuts.

- ■ *The Price Is Right*, hosted by **Bill Cullen**, graduates from daytime to prime time television.

- ■ **Howard Cossell** gets his first regular daily sports wrap-up program.

- ■ **Kermit the Frog** makes his debut on the *Tonight Show*.

# Leave it to Beaver debuts on CBS, beginning a 7-year run.

*TV's Cleaver family: mom Barbara Billingsly, dad Hugh Beaumont, big brother Tony Dow and Jerry Mathers as the Beaver.*

*Lucille Ball*

The *I Love Lucy* gang begins taping one-hour shows called *The Lucy-Desi Comedy Hour*. Meanwhile, Lucille Ball's *Desilu Productions* reaches basic agreement to purchase RKO Studios.

**Elvis Presley** makes final appearance on *The Ed Sullivan Show*.

DJ **Alan Freed** hosts first prime-time rock special, the *Rock 'n' Roll Show*.

Alan Freed

**BORN IN 1957** ★ DAN CASTELLANETA ★ KATIE COURIC ★ FRAN DRESCHER ★ LEEZA GIBBONS ★ MATT LAUER ★ PAUL REISER ★ RAY ROMANO ★ KATIE SAGAL ★ VANNA WHITE

Homer Simpson (voiced by Dan Castellaneta)

*Katie Couric*

When **NAT "KING" COLE**'s television show fails to secure a sponsor, singer **Frankie Laine** crosses TV's color line and forgoes his salary to become the first white artist to appear as a guest. **Mel Torme** and **Tony Bennett** follow, but despite higher ratings, the show still doesn't garner a national sponsor, prompting a bitter Cole to call it quits after 13 months.

# PRIMETIME LINEUP

| | | 7:00 | 7:30 | 8:00 | 8:30 | 9:00 | 9:30 | 10:00 | 10:30 |
|---|---|---|---|---|---|---|---|---|---|
| **SATURDAY** | ABC | Local | Keep It in the Family | Country Music Jubilee | | Lawrence Welk's Dancing Party | | Mike Wallace Interviews | |
| | CBS | Local | Perry Mason | | Dick & the Duchess | Gale Storm Show | Have Gun, Will Travel | Gunsmoke | |
| | NBC | Local | People Are Funny | Perry Como Show | | Polly Bergen Show | Giselle MacKenzie Show | What's It For | Your Hit Parade |
| **SUNDAY** | ABC | You Asked for It | Maverick | | Bowling Stars | Open Hearing | All-American Football Game of the Week | | |
| | CBS | Lassie | Jack Benny/ Bachelor Father | Ed Sullivan Show | | G.E. Theater | Alfred Hitchcock Presents | $64,000 Challenge | What's My Line |
| | NBC | Original Amateur Hour | Sally | Steve Allen Show | | Dinah Shore Chevy Show | | Loretta Young Show | |
| **MONDAY** | ABC | Local | American Bandstand | Guy Mitchell Show | Bold Journey | Voice of Firestone | Lawrence Welk's Top Tunes | | |
| | CBS | Local | Adventures of Robin Hood | Burns and Allen | Arthur Godfrey's Talent Scouts | Danny Thomas Show | December Bride | Studio One in Hollywood | |
| | NBC | Local | The Price is Right | Restless Gun | Tales of Wells Fargo | Twenty-One | Turn of Fate | Suspicion | |
| **TUESDAY** | ABC | Local | Cheyenne/Sugarfoot | | Wyatt Earp | Broken Arrow | Telephone Time | West Point Story | |
| | CBS | Local | Name That Tune | Phil Silvers Show | Eve Arden Show | To Tell the Truth | Red Skelton Show | $64,000 Question | Assignment Foreign Legion |
| | NBC | Local | Nat "King" Cole Show | Eddie Fisher Show/ George Gobel Show | | Meet McGraw | Bob Cummings Show | The Californians | |
| **WEDNESDAY** | ABC | Local | Disneyland | | Tombstone Territory | Ozzie and Harriet | Walter Winchell File | Wednesday Night Fights | |
| | CBS | Local | I Love Lucy | Big Record | | The Millionaire | I've Got a Secret | Armstrong Circle Theatre/ U.S. Steel Hour | |
| | NBC | Local | Wagon Train | | | Kraft Television Theatre | | This is Your Life | |
| **THURSDAY** | ABC | Local | Circus Boy | Zorro | Real McCoys | Pat Boone | O.S.S. | Navy Log | |
| | CBS | Local | Sgt. Preston of the Yukon | Harbormaster | Climax | | Playhouse 90 | | |
| | NBC | Local | Tic Tac Dough | You Bet Your Life | Dragnet | People's Choice | Tennessee Ernie Ford | Lux Show w/ Rosemary Clooney | Jane Wyman Show |
| **FRIDAY** | ABC | Local | Adventures of Rin Tin Tin | Adventures of Jim Bowie | Patrice Munsel Show | Frank Sinatra Show | Date with the Angels | Colt .45 | |
| | CBS | Local | Leave it to Beaver | Trackdown | Dick Powell's Zane Grey Theatre | Mr. Adams & Eve | Schlitz Playhouse | The Lineup | Person to Person |
| | NBC | Local | Saber of London | Court of Last Resort | Life of Riley | M Squad | Thin Man | Gillette Cavalcade of Sports | |

# SYLVANIA'S revolutionary 110° TV tube whittles the bulk from BIG SCREEN portables

### The Slimmest Case

New wide-angle tube cuts 7" from former depth. Case is even slimmer than small-screen sets.

### The Biggest Screen

New 17" (overall diagonal) tube gives you a larger picture than other 17" tubes. You get a full 150 square inches of viewable picture.

### The Clearest Picture

Sylvania's new "S-110" chassis builds added power for extra reach in fringe areas; high voltage assures sharper focus.

## SYLVANIA 17" SLIM JIM PORTABLE

*Here is why Slim Jim is slimmer: Because Sylvania has pioneered the development of this new 110° wide-angle picture tube, Sylvania alone can offer you the newest, slimmest, most compact of all 17" portable TV sets.*

Here's another TV "first" by Sylvania: the biggest picture in portable TV—in a case so slender it rests anywhere! This family-size set adjusts to its surroundings as easily as tiny-screen sets.

Until now, big-screen portables were deep and bulky because ordinary picture tubes are so deep. But Sylvania engineers have developed a powerful, wide-angle tube that whittles away awkward bulk.

Thanks to Sylvania's exclusive 110° Deflection Picture Tube, Slim Jim is slimmer, lower, lighter—a pleasure to look at.

You can own a Sylvania 17" Slim Jim portable for as little as **$139.95\***

*Manufacturer's suggested retail price

New excitement in "personal" radios
**Sylvania's "THUNDERBIRD" 7-Transistor Portable Radio**

New, exciting, trim as a sports car, completely tubeless. Sylvania-engineered to pull in distant stations with a clarity new in "personal" radios. Its 7 tiny transistors last far longer than tubes. Room-filling tone—or optional earphones. Hear it—you'll be amazed!

**SPECIAL INTRODUCTORY OFFER—** with new Sylvania 17" SLIM JIM portables

The exclusive swivel base transforms your Sylvania portable into a console with living-room manners. It swivels the set completely around—a full 360°—angles the picture to your own point of view, makes your favorite chair the best seat in the house.

*For a limited time, this handsomely made swivel base is yours for only* **$4.88\***

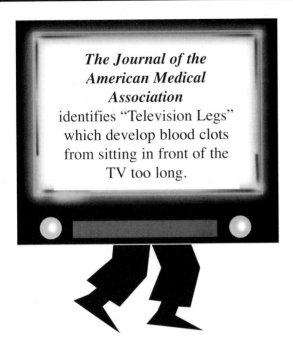

The Journal of the American Medical Association identifies "Television Legs" which develop blood clots from sitting in front of the TV too long.

The FCC accepts applications for pay-TV.

California studios produce 60% of network programming, attracting some of the most talented New York playwrights and actors.

**Charles Van Doren**, champion on the *Twenty-One* quiz show, wins $129,000, lands on the cover of *Time* magazine and receives 500 marriage proposals. Van Doren denies cheating, saying "It's silly and distressing to think that people don't have more faith in quiz shows." It is later revealed in testimony before a Senate subcommittee that he was supplied with answers in advance.

*Truth Or Consequences* is the first videotaped program.

The **Eisenhower/Nixon** inauguration is the first videotaped national broadcast carried by NBC.

A report published in Denmark indicates there are more than 50 million TV receivers in use throughout the world with the United States being the number one user at 38 million and Canada number two at two million. Norway and Bulgaria finish last with 500 receivers each.

# MOST POPULAR TELEVISION PROGRAMS

THE JACK BENNY SHOW
CLIMAX
THE PERRY COMO SHOW
DECEMBER BRIDE
DISNEYLAND
GUNSMOKE
ARTHUR GODFREY'S TALENT SCOUTS
I LOVE LUCY
I'VE GOT A SECRET
MISS AMERICA PAGEANT
PLAYHOUSE 90
THE ED SULLIVAN SHOW
$64,000 QUESTION
UNDERCURRENT
THE LAWRENCE WELK SHOW

*Jack Benny*

# EMMY AWARDS

| | |
|---|---|
| **Best Series:** (one hour) | CAESAR'S HOUR |
| **Best Series:** (half-hour) | THE PHIL SILVERS SHOW |
| **Best Actor In A Series:** | ROBERT YOUNG FATHER KNOWS BEST |
| **Best Actress In A Series:** | LORETTA YOUNG THE LORETTA YOUNG SHOW |
| **Best Comedian:** | SID CEASAR CAESAR'S HOUR |
| **Best Comedienne:** | NANETTE FABRAY CAESAR'S HOUR |

26

# *Radio*

**There are 2,974 AM and 530 FM radio stations in the U.S.**

The first shirt-pocket transistor radio, the Sony TR-63, arrives from Japan.

*When an announcer suddenly quits, young Larry Zeiger gets his first broadcasting opportunity as a morning disc jockey on Miami radio station WAHR. Changing his name to* **LARRY KING***, he also handles afternoon newscasts and sports.*

Vatican radio HVJ goes on the air with a powerful new transmitting station.

| Most Popular Evening Radio Programs | Most Popular Daytime Radio Programs |
|---|---|
| Bob & Ray | Nora Drake |
| Cavalcade Of Stars | Arthur Godfrey |
| Cavalcade Of Sports | My True Story |
| Dragnet | Our Gal Sunday |
| FBI In Peace And War | Ma Perkins |
| Gangbusters | Helen Trent |
| The Great Gildersleeve | Young Doctor Malone |
| Gunsmoke | |
| Heavyweight Championship Fight | |
| Allan Jackson And The News | |
| Monitor | |
| Official Detective | |
| People Are Funny | |
| True Detective Mysteries | |

♪ **The Top 40 music format gains increasing popularity with radio stations across the country.**

**Arthur Godfrey**

Julie Stevens: radio's *Helen Trent*

Harold Peary as *The Great Gildersleeve*

Bob and Ray

"FIBBER MCGEE AND MOLLY" LEAVES THE RADIO AIRWAVES ALONG WITH "GANGBUSTERS," "COUNTERSPY" AND "TRUTH OR CONSEQUENCES."

"THE JACK BENNY PROGRAM" IS REPLACED BY "THE STAN FREBERG PROGRAM."

"LOOK OUT, GRACIE!"

WITH ZENITH SPACE COMMAND TV I CAN CHANGE PROGRAMS FROM ACROSS THE ROOM"...

"George!..You wouldn't dare!"

THE DEAUVILLE, Model A3018

ONLY ZENITH HAS SPACE COMMAND, THE REMOTE CONTROL UNIT THAT TUNES TV BY "SILENT SOUND"...

**JUST TOUCH A BUTTON TO ...**

• shut off the sound of long, annoying commercials while the picture remains on the screen
• turn TV on and off
• change channels 'either direction.

No Wires, No Batteries, No Transistors ...

## NOTHING BETWEEN YOU AND THE SET BUT SPACE!

Now tune TV from your lounge chair ... anywhere in the room! At the touch of a button, the control unit in your hand emits a "Silent Sound" which only the electronic ear of your Space Command receiver can hear. Instantly your set responds! Automatically, each channel comes in sharper than ever before on Zenith's revolutionary new "Sunshine" Picture Tube.

The tone, too, is brilliantly superior, because Zenith's four High Fidelity Speakers, mounted on the sides of your picture screen, fill the room with true "living" sound.

Select the perfect Space Command TV set for your room from Zenith's new Decorator Group in Traditional, Modern, and Provincial style cabinets. You'll have the finest in television plus the joy of Space Command Remote TV Control. Not an extra cost accessory, it's built right into your set!

**BURNS AND ALLEN SHOW**
Seen every week over CBS Television Network

**ZENITH** ZENITH RADIO CORPORATION
Chicago 39, Illinois

The quality goes in before the Zenith name goes on.
Backed for 38 years of leadership in radionics exclusively.
Also makers of Radio, High Fidelity instruments and fine Hearing Aids.

## QUALITY BY Zenith
SPACE COMMAND TV

The Royalty of Television

# *Popular Music*

## '57 HITMAKERS

**Elvis Presley**
Dominating the charts with multiple #1 hits

**Fats Domino**
3 successive #1 R&B hits

3 hits reach #1

**Pat Boone**

**Sam Cooke**
"You Send Me"

**Everly Brothers**
"Wake Up Little Susie," "Bye Bye Love"

**Debbie Reynolds**
"Tammy"

*Jerry Lee Lewis*

*Harry Belafonte*

# 1957 POPULAR SONGS

| | |
|---|---|
| **A Fine Romance** | *Ella Fitzgerald & Louis Armstrong* |
| **All Shook Up** | *Elvis Presley* |
| **April Love** | *Pat Boone* |
| **A White Sport Coat (And A Pink Carnation)** | *Marty Robbins* |
| **Banana Boat Song (Day O)** | *Harry Belafonte* |
| **Blueberry Hill** | *Fats Domino* |
| **Butterfly** | *Andy Williams* |
| **Bye Bye Love** | *The Everly Brothers* |
| **Chances Are** | *Johnny Mathis* |
| **Diana** | *Paul Anka* |
| **Friendly Persuasion** | *Pat Boone* |
| **Honeycomb** | *Jimmy Rodgers* |
| **Jailhouse Rock** | *Elvis Presley* |
| **Little Darlin'** | *The Diamonds* |
| **Love Letters In The Sand** | *Pat Boone* |
| **Magic Moments** | *Perry Como* |
| **Maria** | *from "West Side Story"* |
| **Marianne** | *Harry Belafonte* |
| **Party Doll** | *Buddy Knox* |
| **Peggy Sue** | *Buddy Holly* |
| **Raunchy** | *Bill Justis* |
| **Rock & Roll Music** | *Chuck Berry* |
| **Round And Round** | *Perry Como* |
| **Seventy-Six Trombones** | *from "The Music Man"* |
| **So Rare** | *Jimmy Dorsey Orch.* |
| **That'll Be The Day** | *The Crickets* |
| **The Story Of My Life** | *Marty Robbins* |
| **Tammy** | *Debbie Reynolds* |
| **Tonight** | *from "West Side Story"* |
| **Too Much** | *Elvis Presley* |
| **Wake Up Little Susie** | *The Everly Brothers* |
| **Whole Lot Of Shakin' Going On** | *Jerry Lee Lewis* |
| **You Send Me** | *Sam Cooke* |

Ella Fitzgerald

Peggy Lee

Frank Sinatra

Gene Autry

## Popular Singers
### (A SAMPLING)

**PERRY COMO**
**BING CROSBY**
**EDDIE FISHER**
**PEGGY LEE**
**DEAN MARTIN**
**GISELE MACKENZIE**
**PATTY PAGE**
**FRANK SINATRA**
**ELLA FITZGERALD**

Recently departed from Columbia Records after being forced to record substandard material, FRANK SINATRA sends a telegram to the House Judiciary Sub-committee investigating music industry corruption, accusing Columbia's A&R head MITCH MILLER of soliciting large sums of money from writers whose songs he recorded.

## New Talent

*Paul Anka*
*Patsy Cline*
*Sam Cooke*
*The Crickets*
*Bobby Darin*
*The Everly Brothers*
*Connie Francis*
*Buddy Holly*
*Brenda Lee*
*Jerry Lee Lewis*
*Johnny Mathis*
*Ricky Nelson*
*Conway Twitty*
*Jackie Wilson*

## Top Concert Stars
### (A SAMPLING)

**GENE AUTRY**
**PAT BOONE**
**SMILEY BURNETTE**
**BOB HOPE**
**RICKY NELSON**
**ELVIS PRESLEY**
**JOHNNIE RAY**
**ROY ROGERS**
**JIMMY WAKELY**

♪ **Pat Boone** performs at President Eisenhower's inaugural ball and signs a $1 million television deal.

♪ **Little Richard** shakes up the music world when he announces he is giving up Rock 'n' Roll for religion.

♪ 15-year old Canadian **Paul Anka** writes "Diana," a song dedicated to his childhood babysitter.

♪ The **Everly Brothers'** "Wake Up Little Susie" is banned in Boston because it is thought the song alludes to a sexual affair.

♪ **Buddy Holly and the Crickets** are the first white act to play Harlem's Apollo Theatre in New York.

♪ A first for Rock 'n' Roll— **Sonny James** and **Tab Hunter** both reach No. 1 with "Young Love."

♪ An **Alan Freed** show starring **The Platters**, **The Teenagers** and **Buddy Knox** breaks all attendance records at New York's Paramount Theatre.

♪ 4,000 Rock 'n' Roll fans break through police barriers to greet **Bill Haley** at London's Waterloo Station.

♪ British fans vote **Pat Boone** The World's Outstanding Singer; **Elvis Presley**, World's Outstanding Musical Personality; **Doris Day**, World's Top Female Singer; and **The Platters**, World's Top Group.

*Bill Haley and his Comets*

*Little Richard*

*Buddy Holly and the Crickets*

*Teenagers all over the world love Elvis and show their enthusiasm by buying over sixteen million copies of his eight records and sending him over forty thousand letters a week.*

JOHN LENNON and PAUL McCARTNEY Meet For The First Time At A Church Garden Party.

# Jazz

Miles Davis

*Downbeat's*

## Top Performers

BENNY GOODMAN
COUNT BASIE
LES BROWN
MODERN JAZZ QUARTET
BARNEY KESSEL
RAY BROWN
ERROL GARNER
JIMMY GUIFFRE
MILES DAVIS
HERBIE MANN
ELLA FITZGERALD
FRANK SINATRA
HI-LO'S

Benny Goodman

New releases from Miles Davis, Charles Mingus, Modern Jazz Quartet, Thelonious Monk and Sonny Rollins

**Sonny Rollins** releases a pair of albums, *Way Out West* and *A Night at the Village Vanguard*, featuring the pioneering modern saxophonist accompanied solely by bass and drums. The *Vanguard* album marks the first live recording issued from the legendary New York nightspot.

Idiosyncratic pianist **Thelonious Monk** finally recovers the cabaret card maliciously confiscated by the NYPD in 1951, enabling him to resume club performances. He wastes no time, launching a 6-month residency at the Five Spot with his new quartet which features **John Coltrane** on sax.

**Miles Davis** has disbanded his quintet and embarked on what will prove to be a fruitful partnership spanning several albums with arranger **Gil Evans**. Their first joint endeavor, the adventurous *Miles Ahead*, showcases the trumpeter's work in front of a big band.

**Billie Holiday** *appears on the CBS TV program* The Sound of Jazz, *singing* Fine and Mellow *with support from (l-r)* **Lester Young**, **Ben Webster** *and* **Gerry Mulligan**.

**LOUIS ARMSTRONG** *angrily cancels his U.S. government-sponsored tour of the Soviet Union in protest over America's treatment of southern blacks.*

**JIMMY DORSEY**, jazz clarinetist and famed bandleader who scored 23 hits in the early 1940's dies of cancer at 53 just as his recording of *So Rare* reaches # 2 on the Hit Parade.

## Popular Music

# TOP SELLING COUNTRY RECORDS

**Young Love**
SONNY JAMES

**There You Go**
JOHNNY CASH

**Gone**
FERLIN HUSKY

**A White Sport Coat (and a Pink Carnation)**
MARTY ROBBINS

**Honky Tonk Song**
WEBB PIERCE

**Four Walls**
JIM REEVES

**My Shoes Keep Walking Back to You**
RAY PRICE

**My Special Angel**
BOBBY HELMS

---

### PLEASE MR. TALLY MAN, TALLY ME ROY-AL-TIES

With **Harry Belafonte**'s album *Calypso* one of the biggest selling records in RCA Victor history, do-it-yourself Calypso kits consisting of bongo drums, gourd and maracas sell briskly at $24.50 each.

# DON'T QUIT YOUR DAY JOB

| | |
|---|---|
| Tab Hunter | *Young Love* |
| Robert Mitchum | *Mama Look-a-Boo-Boo* |
| Jerry Lewis | *Rock-a-Bye Your Baby With a Dixie Melody* |
| Anthony Perkins | *A Little Love Can Go a Long, Long Way* |
| Grace Kelly | *True Love* |
| Fess Parker | *Davy Crockett* |

♪ San Francisco poets Lawrence Ferlinghetti and Kenneth Patchen are among poets fusing their poetry with Jazz.

♪ Berry Gordy, Jr. starts Motown Records.

♪ West Indian music becomes the rage in the United States.

♪ Hal David and Burt Bacharach collaborate on their first two big hits—"Magic Moments" and "The Story Of My Life."

## BORN IN 1957 ★

ANITA BAKER ★ LAURA BRANIGAN ★ SHEILA E. ★ GLORIA ESTEFAN ★ VINCE GILL ★ MARLON JACKSON ★ PATTY LOVELESS ★ LYLE LOVETT ★ GEORGE STRAIT ★ DONNY OSMOND ★ EDDIE VAN HALEN ★ SID VICIOUS

*Sheila E.*

35

*When better automobiles are built Buick will build them*

# Solid click on the TROJAN campus

We previewed the B-58 Buick at the University of Southern California — and drew a more enthusiastic turnout than a movie crew on location.

What sent the students the most was that new Miracle Ride, plus Air-Poise Suspension.*

They couldn't get over the way this Buick levels itself, no matter how heavy the load, or where you place it.

They marveled at the way the worst bumps and potholes seemed to disappear beneath the wheels.

And what brought the widest grins of glee was the way this big B-58 sailed up the winding canyon roads without a trace of slew or sway.

When we tallied up the comments, "It's the greatest!" was the mildest.

So — go see what the hubbub's all about, at your Buick dealer's now.

BUICK *Division of* GENERAL MOTORS

*Air-Poise Suspension optional at extra cost on all Series.*

TRY THE MIRACLE RIDE OF—

# THE AIR BORN B-58 BUICK

See TALES OF WELLS FARGO, Monday Nights, NBC-TV and THE PATRICE MUNSEL SHOW, Friday Nights, ABC-TV

# Classical Music

## Europe's New Divas

Anita Cerquetti *(Italy)*
Clara Petrella *(Italy)*
Irene Dalis *(U.S.)*
Eugenia Ratti *(Italy)*

### PASSINGS

*Sibelius*

Finnish composer **JEAN SIBELIUS**, who dropped out of law school to pursue music, is dead at 91.

**ARTURO TOSCANINI**, brilliant Italian conductor who headed La Scala and the Metropolitan Opera, conducting the world premieres of *Pagliacci*, *La Boheme* and *Girl Of The Golden West*, dies at 89.

**BENIAMO GIGLI**, one of the most popular operatic tenors of the century, dies at 71.

**EZIO PINZA**, Metropolitan Opera Basso and Broadway Star, dies at 64.

- Los Angeles Celebrates Igor Stravinsky's 75th Birthday With The Premiere Of *Agon* And *Canticum Sacrum*.

- William Walton Composes *Concerto For Cello And Orchestra*.

- Carl Orff Composes *Comoedia de Christi Resurrectione*.

- Leonard Bernstein Named Musical Director Of The New York Philharmonic.

- Maria Callas Triumphs In Inaugural Concert At New Dallas State Fair Music Hall Opening With An Aria From Mozart's *The Abduction From The Seraglio*.

- Dmitry Shostakovich's *Piano Concerto* Performed In Moscow With Maxim Shostakovich The Guest Soloist.

Famed Cellist **Pablo Casals**, 80, marries his fourth wife, Martita Montañez, a 20-year old student from Puerto Rico.

## OPERA PREMIERES

*Blood Wedding*
**Wolfgang Fortner**
(Cologne)

*Thyl de Flandre*
**Jacques Chailley**
(Brussels)

*Assassinio della Cathedrale*
**Ildebrando Pizetti**
(Milan)

*The Moon And Sixpence*
**John Gardener**
(London)

*The Turn Of The Screw*
**Benjamin Britten**
(Stratford)

*The Portrait*
**Hilding Rosenberg**
(Stockholm)

*Les Dialogues des Carmélites*
**Francis Poulenc**
(Milan)

*Die Harmonie der Welt*
**Paul Hindemith**
(Munich)

*Venus In Africa*
**George Antheil**
(Denver)

**O**ne of the architectural wonders of the world, the Sydney Opera House, *opens, providing a world-class cultural center for theatre, opera and ballet in Australia.*

# Ballet Premieres

## Agon
Igor Stravinsky *(Paris)*

*Stravinsky*

## The Prince Of The Pagodas
Benjamin Britten

## Square Dance
George Balanchine
*New York City Ballet*

## Sebastian
Agnes de Mille
*(An experimental piece performed without music, costumes or sets)*

**T**he Israeli Philharmonic, comprised predominantly of refugees from the Nazis, moves to a new, permanent concert hall in Tel Aviv with **Leonard Bernstein** conducting the opening concert and **Isaac Stern** as guest violinist.

**A**aron Copland composes *Piano Fantasy.*

**G**ian Carlo Menotti's Symphonic Poem *Apocalypse* is performed in Pittsburgh.

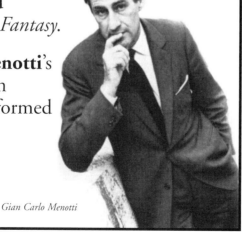

*Gian Carlo Menotti*

**PULITZER PRIZE FOR MUSIC** | Norman Dello Joio *"Meditations On Ecclesiastes"*

*I Could Have Danced, Danced, Danced All Night*

• **W**ith The Growing Popularity Of American Dance, American Ballet Theatre Sponsors Series Of Experimental Performances In New York.

• **N**ew York City Ballet's Prima Ballerina Maria Tallchief Returns After Brief Illness. Among The New Pieces Premiering Are:
"PASTORALE" (Choreographic Debut By Francisco Moncion)
"THE MASQUERS" (Todd Bolender)
"THE UNICORN, THE GORGON AND THE MANTICORE" (Menotti, Choreographed By John Butler)

• **T**he Metropolitan Opera House Hosts The Ballet Russe De Monte Carlo In The Debut Of Several New Works Including "Harlequinade," "The Lady And The Unicorn" And "Sombreros."

*Maria Tallchief*

• **T**he Royal Ballet Visits The Metropolitan Opera House With The Incomparable Margot Fonteyn Dancing In "The Sleeping Beauty," "Swan Lake," "La Péri," "Birthday Offering" And "Petrouchka."

• **T**he Royal Ballet Flies To New York To Perform "Cinderella" On Television With Margot Fonteyn And Michael Somes Dancing The Lead Roles.

• **T**he Renowned Jacob's Pillow Dance Festival Celebrates Its 25th Birthday.

• **A**lwin Nikolais Stages "Runic Canto" And José Limon Produces "Blue Roses" Based On Tennessee Williams' "The Glass Menagerie" At The 10th American Dance Festival Held At Connecticut College.

• **J**osé Limon & Company Begin World Tour Under The Auspices Of The President's International Cultural Program.

DORIS DAY

JOHN RAITT

FIRE NOTICE: route to the stree

SCHRA
IN ROO

S
Co
Se

S

*Showplace*

RADIO CITY MUSIC HALL
Rockefeller Center

Pajama Game *program featuring Radio
City Music Hall Rockettes on cover*

# ON BROADWAY

CHITA RIVERA
& KEN LE ROY
IN LEONARD
BERNSTEIN &
STEPHEN
SONDHEIM'S
**WEST
SIDE
STORY,**
ALSO
FEATURING
CAROL
LAWRENCE
&
LARRY KERT.

# ANOTHER OPENING, ANOTHER NIGHT

Robert Preston and Barbara Cook

## THE MUSIC MAN

## LOOK HOMEWARD, ANGEL
Jo Van Fleet, Anthony Perkins, Arthur Hill

## THE DARK AT THE TOP OF THE STAIRS
Pat Hingle, Teresa Wright, Eileen Heckart

### ROOM AT THE TOP
By John Braine

### ENDGAME
By Samuel Beckett

### THE ENTERTAINER
By John Osborne

### THE CAVE DWELLERS
By William Saroyan

### THE WORLD OF SUSIE WONG
By Richard Mason

- The Thrust Stage Is Introduced At The Stratford Festival Theatre

- Most Successful New Comedy: AUNTIE MAME With Rosalind Russell

Most Successful New Musical: NEW GIRL IN TOWN Based On "Anna Christie"

- Cost Of A Theatre Ticket: $ 1.15 - 4.50

## A VISIT TO A SMALL PLANET
By Gore Vidal

Eddie Mayehoff (*left*) and Cyril Ritchard

# 1957 TONY AWARDS

OUTSTANDING PLAY
**"Long Day's Journey Into Night"**
Eugene O'Neill

OUTSTANDING MUSICAL
**"My Fair Lady"**
Alan Jay Lerner & Frederick Loewe

OUTSTANDING DRAMATIC ACTOR
**Fredric March**
"Long Day's Journey Into Night"

OUTSTANDING DRAMATIC ACTRESS
**Margaret Leighton**
"Separate Tables"

OUTSTANDING MUSICAL ACTOR
**Rex Harrison**
"My Fair Lady"

OUTSTANDING MUSICAL ACTRESS
**Judy Holliday**
"Bells Are Ringing" "My Fair Lady"

OUTSTANDING SUPPORTING OR
FEATURED DRAMATIC ACTOR
**Frank Conroy**
"The Potting Shed"

OUTSTANDING SUPPORTING OR
FEATURED DRAMATIC ACTRESS
**Peggy Cass**
"Auntie Mame"

OUTSTANDING SUPPORTING OR
FEATURED MUSICAL ACTOR
**Sydney Chaplin**
"Bells Are Ringing"

OUTSTANDING SUPPORTING OR
FEATURED MUSICAL ACTRESS
**Edie Adams**
"Li'l Abner"

OUTSTANDING DIRECTOR
**Moss Hart**
"My Fair Lady"

## PASSINGS

MARIA PAVONA CHEKHOVA, devoted sister of
Russian Playwright Anton Chekhov, dies at 93.

---

## Sir Laurence Olivier

**Receives Honorary Doctor's Degree From Oxford University**

## Sir Laurence Olivier

**And His Wife, Vivien Leigh, Lead Protest Against The Destruction Of London's Historic St. James Theatre.**

---

# EUGENE O'NEILL

Dominates The Theatrical Scene With Prizes And Plays Running On And Off-Broadway:

## Pulitzer Prize
**Long Day's Journey Into Night**

## Nobel Prize
**Long Day's Journey Into Night**
(Only American dramatist to have won this most coveted award)

## Drama Critics' Circle Award
**Long Day's Journey Into Night**

## On Broadway
**A Moon For The Misbegotten**

## Off Broadway
**The Iceman Cometh**

O'Neill's Play, **A TOUCH OF THE POET** Scheduled For New York Production Next Year.

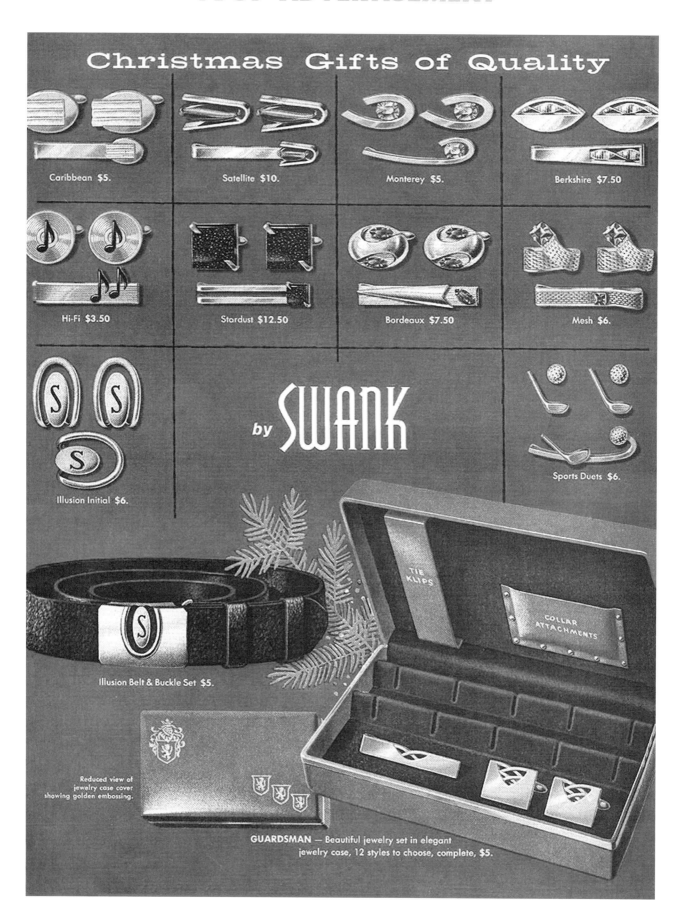

Christmas Gifts of Quality

Caribbean $5.

Satellite $10.

Monterey $5.

Berkshire $7.50

Hi-Fi $3.50

Stardust $12.50

Bordeaux $7.50

Mesh $6.

Illusion Initial $6.

*by* SWANK

Sports Duets $6.

Illusion Belt & Buckle Set $5.

Reduced view of jewelry case cover showing golden embossing.

TIE KLIPS

COLLAR ATTACHMENTS

GUARDSMAN — Beautiful jewelry set in elegant jewelry case, 12 styles to choose, complete, $5.

## NEW WORKS OF NOTE

**JEAN DUBUFFET**
*Mirandoliana* painting

**HENRY MOORE**
*Reclining Figure* sculpture

**PABLO PICASSO**
*Las Meninas* painting

**MARK TOBEY**
*Calligraphy In White*
painting

**MARK ROTHKO**
*Black Over Reds, Red,
White And Brown* painting

**ADOLPH GOTTLIEB**
*Blast I* painting

**WILLIAM BAZIOTES**
*Red Landscape* painting

**ROBERT RAUSCHENBERG**
*Painting With Red
Letter 'S'* painting

**PHILIP GUSTON**
*The Clock, Painter's City*
painting

**ANDREW WYETH**
*Brown Swiss*
painting

**RICHARD DIEBENKORN**
*Girl Looking At
Landscape* painting

**ELLSWORTH KELLY**
*New York, New York*
painting

**HELEN FRANKENTHALER**
*Jacob's Ladder* painting

**SEYMOUR LIPTON**
*Pioneer* sculpture

The Brooklyn Museum holds a showing called *Religious Paintings*, including *Madonna And Child* by **Lorenzo Monaco** with other works by **Veneziano**, **Mantegna**, **Titian**, **Tiepolo**, **Rembrandt**, **Rubens**, **Delacroix** and **Degas**.

The Cleveland Museum of Art holds an exhibition called *The Venetian Tradition* including paintings, drawings and objects d'art dating from the early 16th century to the present day with artists such as **Rubens**, **Piazetti**, **Watteau**, **Delacroix**, **Renoir** and **Cezanne**.

THE LARGEST RARE PRINT EXHIBITION EVER ASSEMBLED IN THE UNITED STATES IS HELD AT THE MINNEAPOLIS INSTITUTE OF THE ARTS WHICH ALSO ARRANGES A LARGE ONE-MAN EXHIBITION OF THE WORK OF CLAUDE MONET IN COOPERATION WITH THE CITY ART MUSEUM OF ST. LOUIS.

## GOING, GOING, GONE

**Gaugin**'s *Still Life With Apples* sells for the highest price ever paid for modern art—$346,170—at a Paris gallery, with **Renoir**'s *Mosque in Algiers* and **Claude Monet**'s *Antibes from the Garden of Salis* selling for $73,228 and $53,650, respectively.

**S**otheby Gallery holds London's biggest sale since 1928, auctioning off **Vincent Van Gogh**'s *Les Usines á Clichy* at $86,800 and his *Head of an Angel* For $72,800.

The Museum Of Primitive Art Sponsored By Nelson A. Rockefeller Opens In New York.

**The Museum Of Modern Art mounts a one-man exhibition of JACKSON POLLOCK, the American Abstract Expressionist painter who died last year.**

New York's Museum of Modern Art and the Art Institute of Chicago organize a **Picasso** 75th Anniversary Exhibition covering 60 years of the artist's work, including pieces from his own collection: *The Pipes Of Pan, Woman Dressing Her Hair, Paul As Harlequin, Portrait Of J.R. With Roses* and *Still Life With Chair Caning.*

An exhibition of the **Joseph Pulitzer, Jr.** Collection is held at the Fogg Museum in Cambridge and the Knoedler Galleries in New York for the benefit of Harvard University, including **Matisse**'s *The Bathers* and **Picasso**'s *Woman In Yellow.*

# ART PRIZES

## The Art Institute Of Chicago

**Eleanor Coen** "Growing City" (painting $1,500)
**Robert Anderson** "Yesterday, Today And Tomorrow" (collage $1,000)
**Richard Hunt** "Steel Bloom" (welded sculpture $750)

## Pennsylvania Academy Of The Fine Arts

**Henry C. Pitz** Winner, The Philadelphia Watercolor Club Medal

## The 4th Biennale At São Paulo, Brazil

**Ben Nicholson** Winner, First Prize For Painting (Also received Guggenheim Award of $10,000)

## Art Institute Of Chicago's 62nd American Exhibition Of Painting And Sculpture

**Seymour Lipton** "The Cloak" (welded sculpture, First Prize: $2,000)
**James Brooks** "R-1953" (Abstract-Expressionism, Second Prize: $1,000)
**Hedda Sterne** "New York" (Abstract, Third Prize: $750)

## Washington's 25th Biennial Exhibition Of Contemporary American Art At The Corcoran Gallery Of Art

**Loren MacIver** "The Street" (First Prize)
**Fritz Glarner** "Recreational Painting No. 79" (Second Prize)
**Josef Albers** "Homage To The Square" ( Third Prize)

New York's Guggenheim Museum has exhibition of **Marcel Duchamp, Raymond Duchamp-Villon** and **Jacques Villon**, three influential French brothers active in the modern movement.

## PASSINGS

FRANTISEK KUPKA, Czech painter who created first totally abstract work.

DIEGO RIVERA, controversial Mexican mural painter, dies at 71.

Rumanian sculptor CONSTANTIN BRANCUSI, known for the beautiful simplicity of his work, is dead at 81.

French artist **JEAN COCTEAU** designs the paintings, altar and all other decorations for a 14th-century chapel in Villefranche-sur-Mer, a French fishing village.

# Books

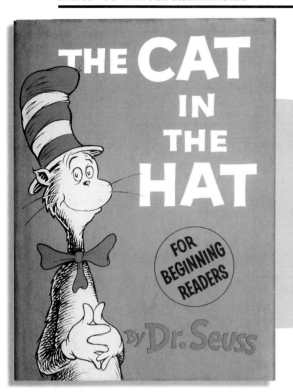

**D**espite receiving many rejections from publishers because of the strange pictures and peculiar rhymes, Theodor Geisel — better known as **Dr. Seuss** — persists and gets a publishing deal for **The Cat In The Hat**, which appears to intrigue adults as much as the wee folks. **How The Grinch Stole Christmas** is also published.

Jack Kerouac's stream-of-consciousness novel **On The Road** gives rise to the words "Beat" and "Beatnik" as popular phrases to describe the "Beat Generation."

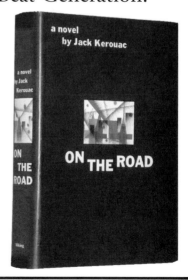

 The NEW CAMBRIDGE MODERN HISTORY Begins Publication.

 JOHN DOS PASSOS Is Awarded The National Institute Of Arts And Letters Gold Medal For Fiction, Awarded Once Every Ten Years.

 Farleigh Dickinson University Begins Publishing THE LITERARY REVIEW: AN INTERNATIONAL JOURNAL OF CONTEMPORARY WRITING.

 200,000 Copies Of FRANÇOISE SAGAN's Third Novel In Four Years, IN A MONTH, IN A YEAR Hits Paris Bookstores.

 ALLEN GINSBERG's U.K.-printed poem HOWL is seized by U.S. customs officials on grounds of obscenity.

# Books

James Agee
   A DEATH IN THE FAMILY

Winston S. Churchill
   A HISTORY OF THE ENGLISH
   SPEAKING PEOPLES, VOL. III
   THE AGE OF REVOLUTION

Kathleen Winsor
   AMERICA WITH LOVE

Bernard Malamud
   THE ASSISTANT

Ayn Rand
   ATLAS SHRUGGED

Edwin Way Teale
   AUTUMN ACROSS AMERICA

Theodor Plievier
   BERLIN

Henry Miller
   BIG SUR AND THE
   ORANGES OF HIERONYMUS
   BOSCH

James Gould Cozzens
   BY LOVE POSSESSED

Dr. Seuss
   THE CAT IN THE HAT

Erskine Caldwell
   CERTAIN WOMEN

Kathleen Kenyon
   DIGGING UP JERICHO

Boris Pasternak
   DR. ZHIVAGO

Leonard B. Meyer
   EMOTION AND MEANING
   IN MUSIC

Robert Bolt
   THE FLOWERING CHERRY

Ian Fleming
   FROM RUSSIA WITH LOVE

James Thurber
   FURTHER FABLES FOR
   OUR TIME

James Baldwin
   GIOVANNI'S ROOM

Jonathan Griffin
   THE HIDDEN KING

Vance Packard
   THE HIDDEN PERSUADERS

Lawrence Durrell
   JUSTINE

Art Linkletter
   KIDS SAY THE DARNDEST
   THINGS

Isak Dinesen
   LAST TALES

Gerald Green
   THE LAST ANGRY MAN

Roger Vailland
   THE LAW

Pearl S. Buck
   LETTER FROM PEKING

Stuart Gilbert, editor
   LETTERS OF JAMES JOYCE

Fred Hoyle
   MAN AND MATERIALISM

Simone de Beauvoir
   THE MANDARINS

Kyle Onstott
   MANDINGO

Mary McCarthy
   MEMORIES OF A
   CATHOLIC GIRLHOOD

Trevor Huddleston
   NAUGHT FOR YOUR
   COMFORT

T.S. Eliot
   ON POETRY AND POETS

## NOBEL

### Literature:

ALBERT CAMUS
(FRANCE)

## PULITZER

### Poetry:

RICHARD WILBUR
*Things Of This World*

### History:

GEORGE F. KENNAN
*Russia Leaves The War*

### Drama:

EUGENE O'NEILL
*Long Day's Journey Into Night*

### Journalism:

CHICAGO DAILY NEWS

### National Reporting:

JAMES RESTON
*New York Times*

### International Reporting:

RUSSELL JONES
*United Press*

### Biography or Autobiography:

JOHN F. KENNEDY
*Profiles In Courage*

Nevil Shute
ON THE BEACH

Jack Kerouac
ON THE ROAD

William Hollingsworth Whyte
THE ORGANIZATION MAN

Edgar Preston Richardson
PAINTING IN AMERICA

Cyril Northcote Parkinson
PARKINSON'S LAW AND
OTHER STUDIES IN
ADMINISTRATION

C. Day Lewis
PEGASUS

Jean Kerr
PLEASE DON'T EAT THE
DAISIES

A.J. Ayer
THE PROBLEM OF
KNOWLEDGE

Max Shulman
RALLY ROUND THE
FLAG, BOYS!

Theodore Draper
THE ROOTS OF
AMERICAN COMMUNISM

Iris Murdoch
THE SANDCASTLE

Saul Bellow
SEIZE THE DAY

John Steinbeck
THE SHORT REIGN OF
PIPPIN IV

Langston Hughes
SIMPLE STAKES A
CLAIM

Chaing Kai-Shek
SOVIET RUSSIA IN CHINA

Irving Wallace
THE SQUARE PEGS

Marshall W. Stearns
THE STORY OF JAZZ

Françoise Sagan
THOSE WITHOUT
SHADOWS

William Faulkner
THE TOWN

Arthur Bryant
THE TURN OF THE TIDE

Richard Hoggart
THE USES OF LITERACY

John Cheever
THE WAPSHOT
CHRONICLE

Robert Paul Smith
WHERE DID YOU GO?
OUT. WHAT DID YOU
DO? NOTHING.

William Saroyan
THE WHOLE VOYAGE
AND OTHER STORIES

James Thurber O
THE WONDERFUL

Richard Mason
THE WORLD OF SUSIE
WONG

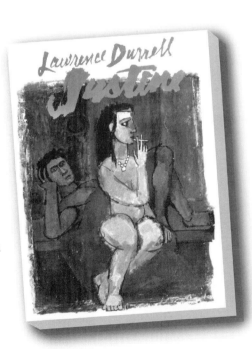

**Laura Ingalls Wilder**, author of *Little House On The Prairie*, dies at 90.

**John Van Druten**, author of *I Remember Mama* and *I Am A Camera*, dies at 56.

**Gabriela Mistral**, Nobel Prize winning Chilean poet dies at 67.

**Nikos Kazantzakis**, Greek novelist who wrote *Zorba The Greek* and *The Last Temptation Of Christ*, dies at 74.

# In The News

*President **Dwight David Eisenhower** is inaugurated for a second term in a public ceremony on January 21, 1957.*

*His inaugural speech is a plea for peace among all nations.*

**"...May the turbulence of our age yield to the true time of peace when men and nations shall share a life that honors the dignity of each..."**

*Ike and Mamie attend post-inaugural festivities with children David and Julie.*

# *Politics and World Events*

## Egyptian/Israeli Impasse Delays Opening of the Suez Canal

l-r: Humphrey, Dulles, Ike, Lodge

**P**resident **Eisenhower**, vacationing at the Georgia plantation of Secretary of the Treasury **George Humphrey**, calls an emergency meeting of his top advisors, including **Henry Cabot Lodge** and **John Foster Dulles**, to discuss the Mid-East crisis. At the heart of the problem is the Suez Canal, still closed as a result of damage and sunken ships following the 1956 Suez military intervention by the U.K., France and Israel opposing Egyptian President **Gamal Abdel Nasser**'s nationalization of the canal.

The President is apprised of the deteriorating situation by Secretary of State Dulles. The gravity of the Egyptian impasse causes him to cut short his winter holiday and return to Washington.

United Nations Undersecretary **Ralph Bunche** arrives in Gaza to monitor the situation.

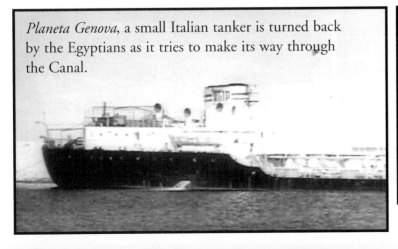

*Planeta Genova*, a small Italian tanker is turned back by the Egyptians as it tries to make its way through the Canal.

The captain of the Italian tanker is told he cannot pass because supposedly the canal has not been cleared of a sunken vessel loaded with explosives.

# The Suez Canal is Finally Cleared for Passage

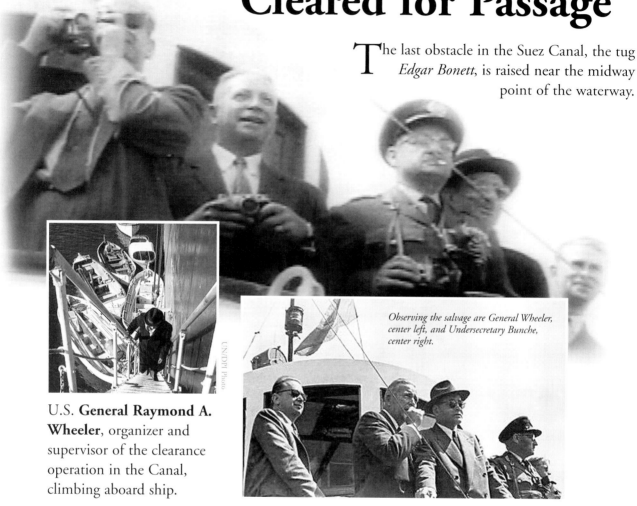

The last obstacle in the Suez Canal, the tug *Edgar Bonett*, is raised near the midway point of the waterway.

U.S. **General Raymond A. Wheeler**, organizer and supervisor of the clearance operation in the Canal, climbing aboard ship.

*Observing the salvage are General Wheeler, center left, and Undersecretary Bunche, center right.*

UN/DPI Photo

Removal of the craft, scuttled five months ago by Egypt, clears the way for passage in the near future, although the questions of tolls and control have still not been resolved.

# Nixon Visits Hungarian Refugee Camps in Austria
## – *SEEKS SPEEDIER AID FOR REFUGEES*

Vice President **Richard Nixon** is welcomed by Austrian dignitaries on his inspection trip to Hungarian refugee centers.

His trip includes visits to all the major collection points where refugees await their final destination. 21,000 refugees are authorized to enter the United States, but Nixon is convinced the number should be increased.

Old and young, they have come to these refugee centers seeking freedom and to try to convince Nixon that America should expand its quota.

Nixon and Tracy Voorhees, head of the refugee program, arrive for a meeting with President Eisenhower after their trip to Austria.

Nixon gives Eisenhower a report on the results of his inspection trip. His recommendation is for more help.

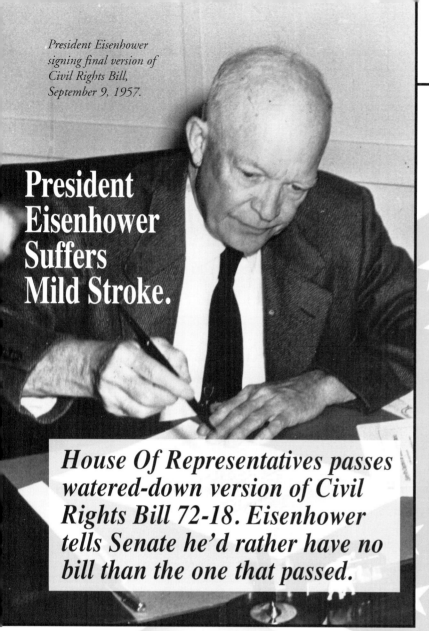

*President Eisenhower signing final version of Civil Rights Bill, September 9, 1957.*

# President Eisenhower Suffers Mild Stroke.

*House Of Representatives passes watered-down version of Civil Rights Bill 72-18. Eisenhower tells Senate he'd rather have no bill than the one that passed.*

# Eisenhower Proposes International Arms Control

## President Eisenhower Signs Niagra Power Bill Authorizing Construction Of Hydroelectric Dam.

## THE U.S. SUPREME COURT

### ...Upholds Ban On Sale Of Obscene Literature. Justices William O. Douglas And Hugo Black Cast Dissenting Votes.

### ...Rules That A License To Practice Law May Not Be Refused On The Grounds Of Past Association With The Communist Party.

## U.S. MILITARY FORCE REDUCED BY 100,000 TROOPS BY SECRETARY OF DEFENSE WILSON.

 **U.S. State Department Refuses To Validate Eleanor Roosevelt's Passport For A Visit To Communist China.**

Nine Democratic Women Hold Seats In The House Of Representatives.

Democrats Win Major Contests In Off-Year Elections.

 **Estes Kefauver Loses Foreign Relations Committee Seat To Senator John F. Kennedy.**

*James R. Hoffa*

## Teamster Corruption Investigated By U.S. Senate.

Teamster V.P. Jimmy Hoffa Arrested By FBI On Bribery Charges.

Jimmy Hoffa Indicted On Charges Of Bribery, Conspiracy And Obstruction Of Justice For Trying To Get Senate Committee Files.

Expelled AFL-CIO Head Dave Beck Charged With Income Tax Evasion.

Teamsters Union Expelled From AFL-CIO When Jimmy Hoffa, With The Full Backing Of The Union, Refuses To Purge The Union Of Criminals.

Jimmy Hoffa Acquitted On Bribery Charges.

New York Mayor Robert F. Wagner, Jr. Wins Re-Election By A Record Margin Of Over 919,000 Votes While Traditionally Republican Up-State New York Goes Democrat Electing Five New Mayors.

William Proxmire, The First Democrat To Be Elected To The U.S. Senate In The State Of Wisconsin In 25 Years, Wins The Seat Vacated By The Death Of Joseph R. McCarthy.

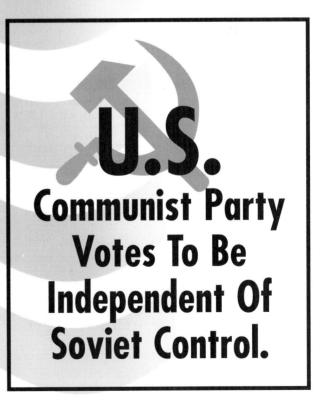

## U.S. Communist Party Votes To Be Independent Of Soviet Control.

## SOUTHERN DISCOMFORT

Interracial athletic events are outlawed by the Georgia State Legislature.

A bomb rips through a Nashville school that admits African Americans.

A black minister in Birmingham is beaten by a mob as he tries to enter a group of children, including his daughter, into an all-white school.

Willie James Edwards is forced by Klansmen to jump to his death from a railroad bridge in Montgomery.

**D**espite a record filibuster lasting 24 hours and 18 minutes by South Carolina Senator **Strom Thurmond** (left), the first major civil rights bill since Reconstruction is passed by the Senate under the leadership of Democrat **Lyndon B. Johnson**. The bill not only assures voting rights for minorities, it also creates a Civil Rights Commission.

> In 1954, the U.S. Supreme Court ruled in Brown vs. Topeka Board of Education that segregated schools are "inherently unequal."

## THE LITTLE ROCK NINE

In September, nine black students—known as the "Little Rock Nine"—enroll at Little Rock, Arkansas' Central High School, touching off one of the key civil rights struggles of the decade. The students face violent protests from jeering, angry mobs of white students and adults, determined to block their entrance. Segregationist Governor Orval Faubus orders the Arkansas National Guard to bar the nine students from attending class. In response, President Eisenhower signs an emergency proclamation calling on all parties to cease and desist and dispatches the 101st Airborne Division to Little Rock to ensure the safe entry of the youngsters.

*President Eisenhower and Arkansas Governor Faubus following a Sept. 14 meeting.*

*The "Little Rock Nine."*

*U.S. troops escort the students to school in October.*

# Russian Spy Arrested In Brooklyn

**Vilyam Genrikhovich Fisher**, a.k.a. **Rudolf Abel**, is arrested after a 9-year spying career for the Russians.

Fisher transported microfilm inside a phony coin container. The affair becomes known as the "Hollow Nickel Case."

Operating from an artist's studio just a stone's throw from the Federal Building, the Russian master spy will be tried in that very building.

# NEW AIR RECORDS SHRINK THE WORLD

**T**his B-52 bomber flys around the world – a distance of 24,000 miles at an average speed of 520 m.p.h. – breaking all existing records.

# GEN. CURTIS LE MAY
## Breaks Non-Stop Record

**T**he jets fly 11,000 miles non-stop from Massachusetts to Buenos Aires in record time of 13 hours, 2 minutes, 51 seconds at a speed of 450 m.p.h.

**G**eneral Curtis E. Le May getting ready to lead a group of jet Strato-Tankers.

# PRIME MINISTER ANTHONY EDEN REPLACED BY HAROLD MACMILLAN

Macmillan

Britain's Prime Minister Anthony Eden's career ends after only 21 months in office, one of the shortest for a Prime Minister in Britain's history. The tragedy of the Suez invasion and ill health bring about his resignation.

Queen Elizabeth II replaces Eden with Harold Macmillan, leader of the right wing Conservative Party who will now have to face Britain's many financial problems and shrinking colonial empire. Son of an American mother, he will carry on the tradition of 10 Downing Street.

Eden

## Germany's Chancellor Adenauer Returned To Office

Enthusiastic well-wishers greet the Chancellor.

In an overwhelming vote of confidence, the Republic of Germany returns 81-year old Chancellor Konrad Adenauer (left) and his government to office.

# CANADA'S ELECTION UPSET

In Canada an upset election ousts Prime Minister Louis St. Laurent and his Liberal government ending his party's 22-year rule.

Winning by a narrow margin, newly installed Prime Minister Diefenbaker and his Conservative Party will be dealing with Canada's expanding economy and industry.

# CRISIS IN JORDAN
## MARTIAL LAW DECLARED AS 6TH FLEET STANDS BY

A young soldier stands guard outside the palace.

The world focuses its attention on the royal palace in Amman, Jordan.

The young King Hussein, facing a political crisis as Jordan's Nasserite government maneuvers to abolish his monarchy, struggles to keep his nation intact. Failing to reach a political solution, he declares martial law.

Loyal Bedouin sheiks pledge their allegiance to Hussein.

Facing the first test of his Middle East doctrine, President Eisenhower proclaims Jordan's independence to be vital.

Implementing the doctrine, heavy elements of the 6th fleet are put to sea under sealed orders for a show of force.

# INDEPENDENCE DAY CELEBRATION IN GREECE

The King and Queen of Greece lead the parade celebrating Greek Independence Day.

The highlight of the parade is young Prince Constantine's first official appearance with his father.

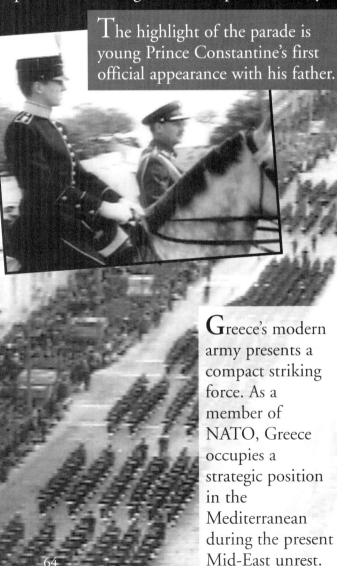

Greece's modern army presents a compact striking force. As a member of NATO, Greece occupies a strategic position in the Mediterranean during the present Mid-East unrest.

# A NEW NATION IS BORN IN IN AFRICA

Vice President and Mrs. Nixon are in Africa to attend ceremonies celebrating Ghana's independence from Britain.

Jubilant natives perform their tribal dance.

Nkrumah Kwame (r), pictured with Harlem Representative Adam Clayton Powell, is the first president of the former British Colony of the Gold Coast.

# The 3ʳᵈ Aga Khan, Mega Millionaire Leader Of 40 Million Ismaili Shia Muslims, Dies At 80.

**M**ourners gather to pay tribute to their beloved leader, Sultan Mahommed Shah of Pakistan.

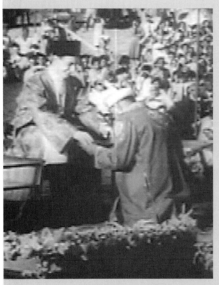

**B**efore his death, the Aga Khan chose his 20-year old grandson, Karim Khan, to be his successor.

**T**he Aga Khan's French wife mourns the loss of her husband.

## Philippine President Ramón Magsaysay, Patriot And Leader Of His People, Dies In Plane Crash On Island Of Cebu. 2 Million Attend His Funeral.

# Missile to Missile

**First U.S. Civilian Atomic Power Plant Goes Into Operation In Shippingport, Pa.**

*The First Test Of An Atlas Intercontinental Missile Ends In Failure When It Explodes Shortly After Take-Off From Its Launching Site In Cape Canaveral, Florida.*

James R. Killian, Jr. Named Special Aid For Space Technology By President Eisenhower.

*U.S. Unveils Plan To Install Intermediate-Range Missiles In Western Europe.*

*U.S. Fails In Three Attempts To Fire Rocket 3,000 Miles Into Space.*

*U.S. Successfully Tests Intermediate-Range Ballistic Missile Jupiter.*

*U.S. Launches The U.S.S. Skate In Groton, Connecticut—Its Third Atomic Powered Submarine.*

**Navy Launches Rocket With Satellite Instruments 126 Miles Into Space.**

## THOR INTERMEDIATE-RANGE MISSILES TO BE PRODUCED BY AIR FORCE.

**Nuclear Test Series Set Off In Yucca Flat, Nevada By U.S. Atomic Energy Commission Including First Underground Test.**

**The Soviet Union Launches *Sputnik*, The First Man-Made Satellite, Into Orbit Around The Earth. President Eisenhower Addresses Nation To Allay Fears Concerning The Soviet's Scientific Achievements.**

**In A Pact With The U.S., Soviets Agree To Place Earth Satellite And All Pilotless Missiles Under International Control. 22 Nations Support U.S. Plan To Limit Outer Space Exploration To Peaceful Purposes Only.**

The Army Air Defense Command Issues Report That New York And Other Major American Cities Will Be Defended By *Nike Hercules* Missiles With Atomic Warheads.

## Soviets Launch LENIN, First Nuclear Ice-Breaker.

**Asserting Soviet Missile Superiority, Khrushchev Challenges U.S. To Rocket-Range Shooting Match.**

## International Atomic Energy Agency Is Formed.

The Soviets Become The First Nation To Ratify International Atomic Energy Agency Charter.

Andrei Gromyko Replaces Dmitri T. Shepilov As Soviet Foreign Minister.

China's Chou En-lai Visits Moscow.

As A Warning To Western Europe Against Nuclear War, The Soviet Union Tests Another H-Bomb.

In A Move To Decentralize Russian Industry, Khrushchev Creates 92 Industrial Regions.

Soviets Agree To Western Plan For Atomic Test Ban.

Soviet Leader Khrushchev Promises Elevation Of Soviet Standard Of Living Stating: "Marxism-Leninism Will Taste Better With Butter."

Tito And Khrushchev Meet In Belgrade Pledging Closer Ties.

Two U.S. Diplomats Expelled From Moscow On Charges Of Spying.

Soviet War Hero Marshal Georgi Zhukov Stripped Of All Power.

**First Russian Warships To Use The Suez Canal Since 1917 Pass Through The Waterway.**

**Members Of The Soviet U.N. Delegation Land At McGuire Air Force Base In New Jersey In First Soviet Civilian Plane To Touch Down In The United States.**

# CUBA & FIDEL CASTRO

Cuban Rebel Leader Fidel Castro Wages Fight Against Fulgencio Batista Regime From Secret Jungle Outpost.

Castro Interviewed On CBS Documentary On Cuban Revolution.

Cuba's President Batista Suspends All Constitutional Guarantees In Response To Outbreak Of Anti-Government Violence.

Castro Joined By Cuban Soldiers In Fighting South Of Havana.

Cuban President Batista Will Not Seek Re-Election.

# INTERNATIONAL HEADLINES

Saudi Arabia's King Saud Visits Washington With Son On Official Visit.

Agreement Regulating Seal Hunting Ratified By The U.S., Soviet Union, Canada And Japan.

U.S. Continues Its Policy Of Non-Recognition Of Red China.

Benito Mussolini's Widow Receives Permission From The Italian Government To Exhume The Coffin Of Il Duce To Hold A Funeral.

François Duvalier Elected President Of Haiti.

French And British Banks Nationalized By Egypt.

Egypt Bars Israel Access To The Suez Canal And Saudi Arabia Cuts Off Gulf Of Aqaba.

Kashmir Becomes Indian State.

American Occupation Headquarters In Japan Is Dismantled.

The U.N. Demands Complete And Unconditional Israeli Withdrawal From The Gaza Strip. Thousands Of Israelis Protest.

Israel Withdraws From The Gaza Strip.

Indonesian President Sukarno Escapes Assassination Attempt In Jakarta.

With U.S. Backing In The Form Of $10 Million In Foreign Aid, Jordan's King Hussein Leads Military Coup Ousting Pro-Egyptian Sympathizers In Government.

Israel Offers To Negotiate With Arabs On Refugee Problem.

Archbishop Makarios Is Released By The British Who Bar Him From Cyprus.

Egypt, Saudi Arabia And Syria Sign Accord To Replace British Aid To Jordan.

Announcement From Jerusalem On The Fall Of Premier David Ben Gurion's Coalition Government.

A Grenade Attack Injures Israeli Premier David Ben-Gurion Along With Four Cabinet Members.

Jordan Closes Embassy In Cairo.

Hungary Institutes Death Penalty For Strikes And Other Acts Of Civil Disobedience.

Three Leaders Of The Hungarian Uprising Sentenced To Death.

Ireland Elects Eamon de Valera As Prime Minister.

French Government Tries To Restore Peace In Algiers.

# GREAT BRITAIN

◆ QUEEN ELIZABETH II OPENS CANADIAN PARLIAMENT, THE FIRST REIGNING MONARCH TO DO SO. THEN ON TO THE U.S. FOR STATE FUNCTIONS INCLUDING VISIT TO WILLIAMSBURG, THE FIRST BRITISH SETTLEMENT.

◆ QUEEN ELIZABETH II ABOLISHES PRESENTATION AT COURT FOR DEBUTANTES.

◆ WOMEN TO SIT IN BRITAIN'S HOUSE OF LORDS FOR THE FIRST TIME IN HISTORY.

◆ MALAYA, THE LAST OF BRITAIN'S ASIAN COLONIES, WINS INDEPENDENCE AND ELECTS FIRST RULER, SIR ABDUL RAHMAN.

◆ PHILIP, DUKE OF EDINBURGH, BECOMES PRINCE OF THE UNITED KINGDOM IN AN ACT BY HIS WIFE, QUEEN ELIZABETH II.

◆ GREAT BRITAIN GRANTS AUTONOMY TO NIGERIA.

## NOBEL PEACE PRIZE

### Lester B. Pearson

Former Secretary of State for External Affairs of
Canada; former President of the 7th Session of the
United Nations General Assembly

Zagreb, Yugoslavia Is The Site Of One Of
The First U.S. Style Supermarkets To Open
In The Eastern Bloc.

**BORN IN 1957**

Princess Caroline
Of Monaco &
Caroline Kennedy

Wisconsin Senator Joseph McCarthy, dies At 48 of hepatitis aggravated by cirrhosis, his political career in ruins. McCarthy spearheaded the anti-communist crusade that leveled accusations of disloyalty against hundreds of Americans and which many decried as a baseless witch hunt.

King Haakon VII of Norway dies at 85, succeeded by his 54-year old son, Olaf V.

*McCarthy*

*Your heart will be glad you came by DC-7*

# Whatever your reason for getting there sooner...

## Take the **DC-7**—world's fastest airliner

With its top speed a remarkable 410 miles an hour, the DC-7 wings you with velvet swiftness across the oceans, across the continents—anywhere in the world!

There's unbeatable luxury and comfort, too. The spacious DC-7 cabin is pressurized, air conditioned, soundproofed and tastefully appointed to make your travel completely restful.

Next trip, get there *sooner*, more *comfortably*—by DC-7. See why *more* people and *more* airlines fly Douglas than all other airplanes *combined!*

# DOUGLAS
### BUILDERS OF THE DC-8 JETLINER

# *People*

Marlon Brando Makes
A Plea For Contributions
To The International
Rescue Committee
To Aid
Hungarian
Refugees.

*"...Give more than you can afford so that the Hungarian people may be reassured that they are not alone..."*

# Dublin's Jewish Mayor Visits Ike

Ireland's unofficial ambassador, Jewish Lord Mayor of Dublin **Robert Briscoe**, visits with Ike at the White House for an informal half hour.

Mayor Briscoe thanks Ike for the kind reception he received in America and for the gift of Irish cut glass—green of course.

# THE MAD BOMBER IS CAUGHT AFTER A 15-YEAR BOMB SPREE

A fifteen-year reign of terror ends in New York when **George Metesky** is captured. The "Mad Bomber" admits to bombing 21 public places between 1940 and 1956 as revenge over being denied a disability pension. His activities caused a number of injuries. Found insane in April, he is committed to Matteawan State Hospital.

**LIDO**

Célébrities Crowd Opening of New Revue at the **LIDO** in **Paris**

Salvador Dali

The Duke & Duchess of Windsor

Françoise Sagan

Maurice Chevalier

Yves Montand & Simone Signoret

The Spicy New Show is an Instant Hit.

The glamour and excitement of New York's social season is enhanced by India's Mrs. Aga Khan (née Joan Lady Camrose) who arrives at the swank Waldorf Astoria to preside over a ball to raise funds for the Musician's Emergency Fund for hospitalized vets of the Musician's Union.

# Gala Ball For Veterans

*A spanking new 1957 car is the grand prize.*

The guest of honor dancing with Prince Oberlinsky.

Wearing over one million dollars in diamonds, Mrs. Khan reigns over one of the most glittering social events of the season.

# Queen Elizabeth & Prince Philip Visit America

**Q**ueen Elizabeth and Prince Philip are greeted at the White House by Ike and First Lady Mamie Eisenhower.

**W**all Street rolls out the red carpet for the young Monarch with an extra special ticker tape parade.

**P**rince Philip chats with Mamie.

**A** water display in New York Harbor for the Queen's enjoyment.

**A** smiling Queen watches the waterworks.

**W**all Streeters line the sidewalks to catch a glimpse of her royal face.

75

Paris is filled with excitement as it anticipates the visit of Queen Elizabeth II.

# Queen Elizabeth Visits Paris

Queen Elizabeth and Prince Philip are the guests of honor at a state dinner.

The first visit by a Royal Monarch in twenty years is jam-packed with ceremonial events. Here the Queen lays a wreath at the Tomb of the Unknown Soldier.

Speaking in French, the Queen makes a toast thanking her host for such a warm and gracious reception.

# Queen Elizabeth Flies to Portugal to End Rumors of a Royal Rift

Prime Minister Macmillan accompanies Queen Elizabeth as she gets ready to fly to Portugal to reunite with Prince Philip.

The Duke of Edinburgh has been on a round-the-world trip and has been separated from the Queen for four months, the longest separation in their 10-year marriage, giving rise to speculations of domestic difficulties.

# In The Fabled Kingdom Of Monaco, A New Princess Has Arrived.

The tiny Princess being held during the christening.

Princess Grace and Prince Ranier III, the proud parents, emerge from the church holding Caroline for her first public appearance.

*In celebration of the birth of Princess Caroline, Prince Rainier III declares amnesty for all prisoners incarcerated for minor infractions.*

*In a bulletin from the Palace, Princess Grace of Monaco announces that, contrary to rumors, baby Princess Caroline does not suck her thumb or any other fingers and that she dislikes hats and having her picture taken.*

*Princess Grace*

Crowds gather to celebrate the christening of Princess Caroline.

With another Royal arrival expected in March, everyone's rooting for a boy.

## Prince Charles Becomes The First British Heir To The Throne To Enter A Preparatory School.

### IS THIS ANY WAY TO TREAT A PRINCE?

Prince Charles, Heir To The British Throne, Enters Cheam School Where He Will Share An Unheated Dorm With Seven Boys, Sleep On A Wooden Springless Bed, Get Caned For Misconduct And Be Limited to 35¢ A Week Spending Money.

*The Duke & Duchess Of Windsor Negotiate To Buy A Burial Plot At Baltimore's Exclusive Green Mount Cemetery.*

Queen Mother Elizabeth, Royal Chancellor of London University, bestows an honorary Doctor of Music degree upon her daughter, Rock 'n' Roll devotee, Margaret.

*Princess Margaret*

**After reviewing the Royal phone bills which amounted to $70,000 annually, Queen Elizabeth decides to install pay telephones in Buckingham Palace to cut down on the high costs.**

After studying a mountain of evidence including the testimony of anthropologists who compared her facial structure to photographs of the teenager, the 83rd Civil Chamber of the West Berlin District Court rules that ANNA ANDERSON is not ANASTASIA, the Romanov Princess who supposedly was the only member of the Royal Family to escape Bolshevik bullets, and has no legitimate claim to the late Russian Czar's fortune.

*Anna Anderson*

Unhappy With Graham Sutherland's Portrait Of Her Husband Winston, Lady Churchill Puts A Match To It With Winnie Concurring That It Makes Him Look Half-Witted.

• • • • • • • • • • • • • • • • • • • • • • •

Sir Winston Churchill's Eldest Daughter Diana Separates From Her Husband Duncan Sandys After 21 Years Of Marriage.

• • • • • • • • • • • • • • • • • • • • • • •

Harry & Bess Truman Leave Independence, Missouri To Visit Their New Grandson, Clifton Truman Daniel With Baseball Mitt In Hand. When Asked If He Would Like The Baby To Be President Some Day, The Ex-President Replied That "He Wouldn't Wish That On Anyone..."

• • • • • • • • • • • • • • • • • • • • • • •

*A.F.L.-C.I.O. United Auto Workers Gets Approval From Harry S. Truman To Purchase His Birthplace House In Lamar, Missouri For Conversion To A National Museum.*

At Over 89 1/2 Years Old, Rhode Island's Democratic Senator Theodore Francis Green Becomes Oldest Man To Ever Serve In The U.S. Congress.

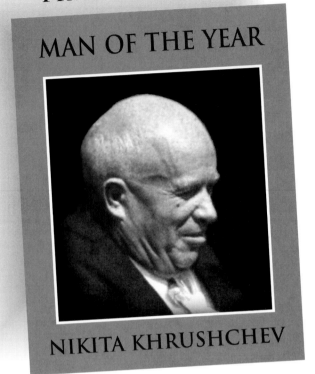

## TIME MAGAZINE
## MAN OF THE YEAR

### NIKITA KHRUSHCHEV

**Ernest Hemingway's dog, *Machakos*, is shot by Cuban soldiers searching for a rebel fugitive.**

## Frank Lloyd Wright
### Interviewed On "Mike Wallace Interviews" Show.

### MAY YOUR NEXT HOUSE FALL DOWN ABOUT YOUR EARS!
Infuriated That One Of His Structures Known As The Robie House Is Going To Be Torn Down To Build A Dormitory For The Chicago Theological Seminary, 87-Year Old Frank Lloyd Wright Declares That Such Destruction Could Only Take Place In America.

## AMERICA'S RICHEST MEN OR... BUDDY, CAN YOU SPARE A MILLION?

| | |
|---|---|
| Sid W. Richardson | $700 Million |
| J. Paul Getty | $700 Million |
| Arthur Vining Davis | $450 Million |
| Henry Ford II | $400 Million |
| Joseph Newton Pew Jr. | $350 Million |
| Howard Hughes | $350 Million |
| Clint Murchison | $300 Million |
| Paul Mellon | $250 Million |
| August A. Busch Jr. | $250 Million |
| John Davison Rockefeller III | $250 Million |
| Robert Winthrop Woodruff | $200 Million |

## AMERICA'S RICHEST WOMEN LADY, CAN YOU SPARE A GIVENCHY?

MRS. HORACE DODGE, Sr.
DORIS DUKE
MRS. ALFRED DuPONT
MRS. EDSEL FORD
MRS. FREDERICK GUEST
MRS. CHAUNCEY McCORMICK
MRS. MERRIWEATHER POST
MRS. C.S. PAYSON
MRS. MARY G. ROEBLING
HELENA RUBINSTEIN

## AMERICAN WOMEN PICK THE MOST INTERESTING MEN ALIVE

Sir Winston Churchill

John F. Kennedy

Bishop Fulton J. Sheen

Dag Hammarskjold

Henry Cabot Lodge, Jr.

Major Charles E. Yeager

Leonard Bernstein

Alfred Hitchcock

Paul Anderson

Peter Freuchen

Bobby Morrow

Frank Gifford

Mickey Mantle

Tab Hunter

Tony Trabet

Frank Sinatra

Albert Schweitzer

President Eisenhower

Edward R. Murrow

Toni Sailer

Dr. Harold Taylor

Roger Bannister

Pablo Picasso

Duke Of Edinburgh

Jose Greco

Harry Belafonte

Alfonso De Portago

Arthur Godfrey

Bing Crosby

Elvis Presley

Liberace

# COUPLING

Alan Alda & Arlene Weiss 💚 John Derek & Ursula Andress 💚 John Carradine & Doris Rich 💚 Bing Crosby & Kathryn Grant 💚 Linda Darnell & Merle Roy Robertson 💚 Anthony Franciosa & Shelley Winters 💚 Rex Harrison & Kay Kendall 💚 Howard Hughes & Jean Peters 💚 Jill Ireland & David McCallum 💚 Martin Landau & Barbara Bain 💚 Sophia Loren & Carlo Ponti 💚 Lee Remick & William Colleran 💚 Elizabeth Taylor & Michael Todd 💚 Francois Truffaut & Madeleine Morgenstern 💚 Robert Wagner & Natalie Wood 💚 Henry Fonda & Contessa Afdera Franchetti 💚 Susan Hayward & Floyd Eaton Chalkley 💚 T.S. Eliot & Esme Valerie Fletcher 💚 Lady Iris Mountbatten & Michael N. Bryan 💚 Harry Belafonte & Julie Robinson 💚 Don Larsen & Corrine Audrey Bress 💚 Marlon Brando & Anna Kashfi 💚 Nanette Fabray & Ranald MacDougall 💚 Lee J. Cobb & Mary Hirsch

# UNCOUPLING

Elizabeth Taylor & Michael Wilding ∽ Lana Turner & Lex Barker ∽ George Sanders & Zsa Zsa Gabor ∽ David Lean & Ann Todd ∽ Brigitte Bardot & Roger Vadim ∽ Ginger Rogers & Jacques Bergerac ∽ Ingrid Bergman & Roberto Rosselini ∽ Gene Kelly & Betsy Blair ∽ Michael Caine & Patricia Baines ∽ Rex Harrison & Lilli Palmer ∽ Frank Sinatra & Ava Gardner ∽ Harry Belafonte & Frances Marguerite Byrd Belafonte ∽ Judy Holliday & David Oppenheim ∽ Frank Loesser & Mary Alice Loesser ∽ Aly Khan & Rita Hayworth ∽ Jack Webb & Dorothy Towne ∽ Edith Piaf & Jacques Pills

## Guess Who's Not Going To Be Bringing Home The Bacon?

*An Australian judge grants a woman a divorce on the grounds that on returning home early from her vacation, she found her husband in bed with another woman, who, mistaking her for the maid, ordered bacon and eggs.*

---

### DEAR ABBY

*Pauline Phillips celebrates her first anniversary as Abby Van Buren, the fastest rising lonelyhearts columnist in the U.S. Syndicated in 80 papers, she is now ranked fourth after Dorothy Dix, Mary Haworth and sister, Ann Landers.*

JACKIE GLEASON and his date are asked to leave Manhattan's swanky Stork Club because of their unruly behavior.

**HEDY LAMARR QUITS HOLLYWOOD IN PROTEST OVER THE NON-CHALLENGING ROLES IN WHICH SHE IS CAST.**

*EARTHA KITT dines with Indian Prime Minister JAWAHARLAL NEHRU as part of her around-the-world quest for truth, meaning and knowledge.*

*Sal Mineo tries a career as a Rock 'n' Roll Singer.*

**Abbott & Costello**, broke and beset with tax problems, split up.

Bickering comedy duo Dean Martin and Jerry Lewis break up.

*Refusing to acknowledge Sophia Loren and Carlo Ponti's Mexican marriage by proxy, the Vatican attacks the couple, accusing them of living in sin and threatening excommunication.*

Colonel and veteran of 20 combat bomber missions over Germany in World War II, actor JAMES STEWART is nominated for promotion to Brigadier General.

Showgirl/actress Marie "The Body" McDonald's hysterical claim of being kidnapped, doped, raped and left in the California desert is thought to be a Hollywood stunt.

**In Memphis, ELVIS PRESLEY reports for an army pre-induction exam in January, 1957. He receives his draft notice over the Christmas holidays.**

# The Perfect 10 Face

The Caricaturists Society of America announces the perfect composite female face:

| | | |
|---|---|---|
| EYES: | Elizabeth Taylor | (Violet, Limpid) |
| FOREHEAD: | Kim Novak | (White, Smooth, Pure) |
| MOUTH: | Anita Ekberg | (Ripe, Sultry, Suggestive) |
| NOSE: | Teresa Brewer | (Cute, Slightly Turned Up) |
| HAIR: | Sophia Loren | (Silky, Soft) |
| CHIN: | Natalie Wood | (Firm, Round & Cute) |
| NECK: | Barbara Ann Scott | (Slender, Strong) |
| EYEBROWS: | Maria Callas | (Sulky, Passionate) |
| EARS: | Helen Stevenson Meyner | (Delicate, Small) |

## BODY CLINCHING OF A DIFFERENT KIND

Former Middleweight boxing champ JAKE LaMOTTA is convicted on charges of aiding and abetting a 14-year old prostitute to hustle "Johns" in his Miami bar.

Clare Booth Luce Receives The University Of Notre Dame's Laetare Medal For Her Brilliant Career.

*Serving a life sentence for killing his wife, Dr. Sam Sheppard is informed that a convict and drug addict named Donald Wedler has confessed to the brutal crime, but that police have discounted the confession.*

*In His Unrelenting Battle Against Smoking, Well Known Surgeon Alton Ochsner Advocates Legal Prohibitions Of Cigarettes If The Number Of Lung Cancer Victims Continues To Increase At The Current High Rate.*

10-Year Old Robert Strom Wins Record Sum Of $224,000 On TV's "The $64,000 Question."

# PASSINGS

**Grace Goodhue Coolidge**, beloved First Lady during her husband **Calvin**'s presidency, dies at 78.

**George "Bugs" Moran**, survivor of the 1929 Valentine's Day Massacre, dies at 64 in Fort Leavenworth Federal Prison.

**Notorious "Murder Inc." figure Albert Anastasia** is gunned down in a New York barber shop at 55.

*Albert Anastasia*

**Elliott Ness**, organizer and leader of the "Untouchables," a squad of nine honest agents assigned to overthrow organized crime, including Al Capone's gang, dies at 54.

**Frank Gannett**, who built a news empire consisting of 22 papers, four radio stations and three TV stations, dies in New York at age 81.

**Herbert Pulitzer**, only surviving son of late editor Joseph Pulitzer, dies at 61.

## YOU SICK?
No scents in that!

Specially for YOU

**King-Size Birthday Card:** ▶

Opens to a foot and a half of wishes for the biggest birthday ever. A Norcross exclusive, in your dealer's special rack. Price $1.00.     Shown is #100HB993.

▲ **Queen-Size Convalescent Card:**

Stands 12 inches high, for an extra measure of "Get Well" cheer. Look for this Norcross extra in its special rack at your dealer's. Price 50 cents. Shown is #50CN700.

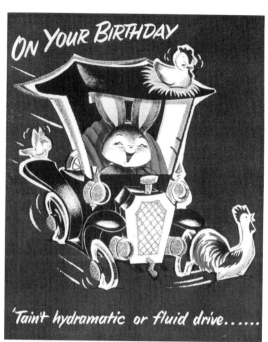

'Taint hydramatic or fluid drive.......

# There's a message here for someone you know

There's someone you can make happier today by saying "I'm thinking of you." Your thoughts, warmly and sincerely expressed in Norcross greeting cards will make you dearer to those you care about.

Whether you say "Happy Birthday," "Get Well," "Congratulations," or just "Hello," Norcross greeting cards say what you want to say. See the beautiful selection —from 5¢ to $1.00—displayed at your Norcross dealer's. You'll be delighted with the many wishes, said in so many pleasing ways.

## NORCROSS **N**
## GREETING CARDS
Say the things you want to say

©NORCROSS, INC.

# Human Interest

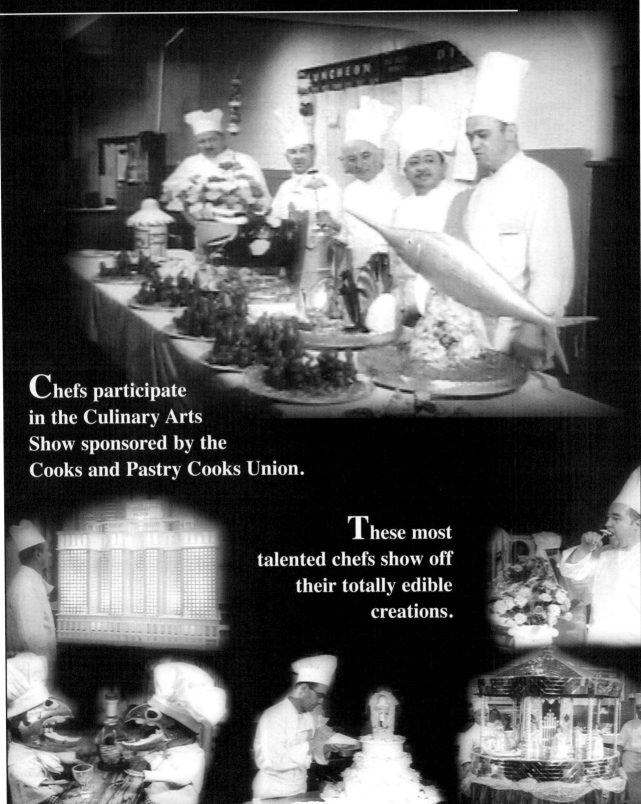

**C**hefs participate
in the Culinary Arts
Show sponsored by the
Cooks and Pastry Cooks Union.

**T**hese most
talented chefs show off
their totally edible
creations.

# PLATYPUSES COME TO AMERICA

New York's Bronx Zoo built a special tank to house three Platypuses sent from Australia – the only ones in captivity in the U.S.

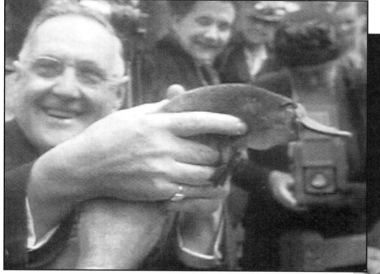

A happy zookeeper gives a smiling welcome as he holds one of these odd little fellows.

In any case, these kids are having a great time with a new-found playmate.

The Platypus is a mammal that lays eggs, swims like a fish, looks like a beaver and is a puzzlement to scientists.

**H**igh school students in Houston, Texas practice Super Yo-Yo or Cheer-E-O, a revised form of yo-yo brought down from Canada by nine Canadian champs.

**T**he Canadian visitors demonstrate the technical difference between the two pastimes.

**E**xperts say that Cheer-E-O with its smoother axle and better balance is a top notch sporting device.

# TEXAS YO-YO CRAZE

**C**laiming an endless array of tricks, the experts demonstrate some of the most popular ones including "The Magic Twirl."

The heroic efforts of Long Island, New York neighbors, firemen and volunteers pay off and after a little more than a day Benny is freed.

**L**ittle Benny Hooper is trapped at the bottom of a 20-foot well and rescuers begin the task of digging him out.

# BOY RESCUED FROM WELL

**B**ennie's anxious mother.

**W**ith the resiliency of youth, Benny, in an oxygen tent, comes through his ordeal with very little injury.

Three Air Force Stratofortresses Complete A 45-Hour World Flight At Average Speed Of 500 M.P.H.

Celebrating Lindbergh's Historic Flight, The "Spirit Of St. Louis II" Flies The Atlantic In 6.7 Hours.

Commercial Air Service Begins Between Tokyo And Copenhagen, Flying Over The North Pole.

The Longest Single-Engine Jet Non-Stop Flight From London To Los Angeles Is Flown By Three U.S. Air Force Pilots.

A U.S. Navy Jet Sets A New Speed Record Of 3 Hours, 22 Minutes, 50.05 Seconds In A Cross-Country Flight From Los Angeles To New York.

The United States Air Force Celebrates Its 50th Birthday.

Major John Glenn Sets A New Transcontinental Record In A Navy BV-1P Voight Crusader – 3 Hours, 23 Minutes, 8.4 Seconds.

---

Civil Defense Officials Predict 2,339,012 Deaths In The Event Of A Nuclear Attack On New York.

Levittown, Long Island Is Thriving Community After First Ten Years Since Its Construction.

Under Heavy Police Guard, The First Black Family Moves Into The White Suburban Community Of Levittown, New York.

---

New York's Madison Square Garden Is The Site Of Billy Graham's Opening Evangelist Crusade.

100,000 Devotees Pack Yankee Stadium To Hear Billy Graham's Sermon.

---

Pope Pius Gives Catholics Permission To Take Pain Pills.

Federal Trade Commission Cracks Down On False Claims On Arthritis Pain Ointments.

---

*Mayflower II*, A Replica Of The Original Ship, Sails From England To Plymouth, Mass. In 53 Days.

The Remains Of Captain Bligh's *Bounty* Found Off Pitcairn Isle.

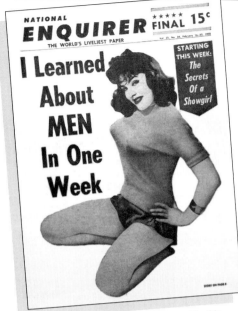

The *New York Evening Enquirer* is renamed the *National Enquirer.*

## SO MUCH FOR ROCK HUDSON & JOHN WAYNE

Oxford University's Union Society Votes In Favor Of A Motion To Resist The Influence Of American Culture On Their Way Of Life.

*Colliers* magazine and *Woman's Home Companion* cease publication.

Professor Reuben Hill Of The Institute Of Research In Social Sciences At The University Of North Carolina Claims That Despite The Growing Divorce Rate And Increased Juvenile Delinquency, The American Family Is Not Breaking Up Because The Quality Of Interpersonal Skills Has Vastly Improved.

Los Angeles Revises Its Building Code, Allowing Construction Of High-Rise Buildings Using Earthquake Stress Engineering.

*According To A Chicago Psychologist, Parents Can Keep Their Children From Developing Anti-Social Behavior By Whispering Loving Words In Their Ears As They Sleep.*

Juvenile Delinquency Reaches Epidemic Proportions Around The World.

Major Crime In U.S. Rises By 7.5% According To Director Of The F.B.I., J. Edgar Hoover.

The Harry S. Truman Library Opens In Independence, Missouri.

A U.S. Flag Flies For The First Time On Wilkes Land, Antarctica.

A 2,400 Mile Telephone Cable Linking California And Hawaii Is Placed In Operation.

Construction Of Entrance Channels And Jetties Begins In Marina del Rey, California.

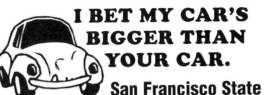

**I BET MY CAR'S BIGGER THAN YOUR CAR.** San Francisco State College Semantics Expert Dr. S. I. Hayakawa Calls New Cars Symbols Of The Male Sex.

- THE AVERAGE CAR GENERATES ENOUGH HEAT IN NORMAL CITY DRIVING SPEEDS TO MAINTAIN A TEMPERATURE IN THE WINTER OF 70 DEGREES IN A 24-ROOM HOUSE.

- DETROIT PHYSICIAN DR. ALBERT D. RUEDEMANN, JR. RECOMMENDS THAT CARS BE EQUIPPED WITH FRONT SEAT HEADRESTS TO PREVENT NECK INJURIES IF A CAR IS REAR-ENDED.

## The 6-Lane Major Deegan Expressway Opens In New York.

ACCORDING TO METROPOLITAN LIFE INSURANCE COMPANY AMERICAN FAMILIES ARE GETTING BIGGER, WITH COUPLES NOW HAVING A THIRD OR FOURTH CHILD.

*In 58% Of American Families, Wives Either Share Or Have A Dominant Role In Handling The Family Finances.*

## IF I WAS A RICH MAN...

Four Out Of Five American Men Would Continue To Work Even If They Inherited A Large Sum Of Money.

So, as I was saying to me...well me, what do you want for dinner...Chinese or Italian?

According To A Visiting Professor Of Psychology At The University Of California, The Measure Of Human Intelligence May Be Our Ability To Talk To Ourselves.

## RIKERS ISLAND

27 Prisoners In Rikers Island Penitentiary Receive Reduced Sentences For Heroic Efforts In Rescuing Victims Of An Airplane Crash During A Blinding Snowstorm.

**Secretary Of The Interior Fred A. Seaton Designates 9,000,000 Acres Of Land In Northeast Portion Of Alaska As A Preserve For Scientific Wildlife Studies And Recreation.**

59 Nations Participate In The U.S. Trade Fair In New York.

### STRIKES

*36-Day Tugboat Strike Hits New York Harbor.*

**Six Major Boston Newspapers Go On Strike.**

♦ **The Supreme Court Rules That First Amendment Protection Does Not Extend To Obscene Material.**

♦ **A New York Judge Releases Allen Ginsberg's "Howl" After The Books Are Seized By Police As Obscene Material.**

## THE POPE REDUCES TO THREE HOURS THE FASTING TIME BEFORE RECEIVING HOLY COMMUNION.

## KENYA GETS ITS FIRST AFRICAN ROMAN CATHOLIC BISHOP.

Buddhist Pilgrims Converge On Katmandu, Nepal To Celebrate The 2,500th Anniversary Of The Death Of Buddha.

### SAY "I DO" OR DIE... SOONER THAN LATER

**Statisticians Of The Metropolitan Life Insurance Company Report That Married Men Live Longer With Death Rate For Single Men 50% Higher Before Age 45. The Difference In Mortality Is Not As Dramatic Between Married And Single Women, However.**

### PASS THE BUTTER...
#### I MEAN MARGARINE

Margarine Exceeds Butter For The First Time In Per Capita Consumption.

### THE LADY IS NOT FOR BURNING

**The 1692 Witchcraft Convictions Of Six Salem Women Are Reversed By The Governor Of Massachusetts.**

## They Don't Do Windows

Heirs to William Randolph Hearst's 120-acre unmanageable San Simeon estate, a repository for what might be described as an art collection bordering on maniacal megalomania, decide to turn it over to the State of California, with the proviso it be declared a historic monument and memorial to Hearst and his mother, Phoebe.

### WE WON'T DO WINDOWS, DISHES, MAKE BEDS, VACUUM OR ANYTHING ELSE FOR THAT MATTER

While 8 Out Of 10 Adolescent American Girls Want To Grow Up And Be Like Their Mothers, They Definitely Do Not Want To Do Housework And While 94% Of Young Girls Want To Get Married, Only 3% Would Consider Being Full-Time Housewives.

14,000 Blacks And Whites Gather At Washington, D.C.'s Lincoln Memorial On A Prayer Pilgrimage For Freedom, Marking The Third Anniversary Of The Supreme Court's Desegregation Decision.

### "Gimme A Double Malted On The Rocks…With A Pretzel Stick"

According To A Yale Center Of Alcohol Studies Report Published In The Journal Of The American Medical Association, Alcoholism Is Virtually Unknown Among Orthodox Jews Due To The Symbolic And Sacred Character Of The Use Of Alcohol. The Orthodox Jew Experiencing Emotional Problems Would Be More Apt To Work Excessively, Gamble Or Seek Another Outlet.

U.S. Postmaster Halts Saturday Mail Delivery Until President Eisenhower Signs Bill Providing An Additional $41,000,000 Appropriation.

The Postmaster General Establishes The Citizens Stamp Advisory Committee To Evaluate The Merits Of New Stamp Proposals.

Despite The Decline In The Number Of Fully Qualified Geishas, The Girls Are Earning More Money Than Ever, Averaging $200 Per Month.

A Visiting Beekeeper At The Rio Claro Apiary In Africa Accidentally Releases 26 Colonies Headed By Extremely Aggressive African Queens.

### HOW DO I HATE THEE, LET ME COUNT THE WAYS…
Researchers At The University Of California, Los Angeles, Come Up With The Most Common Reasons For Marital Failure:
*(1) Adolescent Behavior (2) Unconscious Anti-Marriage Feelings (3) Egocentric (4) Homosexual Tendency Or Male Passivity (5) Sexual Dissatisfaction & Projection (6) Rebellion Against Femininity (7) Flight Into Rejection*

75% Of Students Polled By The New York Herald Tribune Said They Like School.

## ANNUAL COLLEGE COSTS

Public College ... $1,500 Tuition & Living Expenses
Private ........ $2,000 Tuition & Living Expenses

### YALE UNIVERSITY RAISES ITS UNDERGRADUATE TUITION TO $2,000, THE THIRD INCREASE SINCE WORLD WAR II.

### COPY THE CAT

President Of The American Veterinary Radiology Society States That More And More Dogs Are Developing Ulcers Due To The Pressure Of Urban Living – Traffic, The Barking Dog Next Door, Rough Handling By Children. The Solution: Copy The Behavior Of Cats Who Are Much More Relaxed And Don't Get Themselves Upset Over Little Things.

# NEW *WORDS* &

### Asian Influenza
A Different Strain Of Type A.

### Crane Helicopter
A Helicopter Equipped With A Crane For Heavy Lifting.

### Curtain-Wall School
A School With Movable Walls.

### Blast-Down
A Rocket Ship Landing.

### Bombardier
A Bomb-Shaped Vehicle Mounted On Skis For Snow Travel.

### Borazon
A Synthetic Diamond-Like Substance.

### Flying Seat
An Ejection Seat Designed By Lockheed.

### Little Europe
The Six European Nations Comprising The Common Market: France, West Germany, Italy, Belgium, The Netherlands And Luxembourg

### Calypsomania
Addiction To Calypso Music.

### Mailster
A Three-Wheel Scooter For Mailman

### Meter Maid
A Woman Attached To The Police Force To Write Tickets For Parking Meter Violations.

# EXPRESSIONS

### Rockabilly
A Combination Of Country And Rock Sounds.

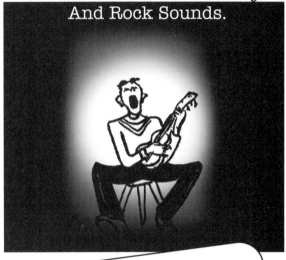

### Stratospheric Drip
Fallout.

### Subliminal Projection
Advertising Designed To Reach The Unconscious Of The Viewers.

### Scuba
Self-Contained Underwater Breathing Apparatus.

### Skort
Combination Skirt And Shorts.

### Teleprompted
Aided By A Teleprompter.

### Total Theatre
A Theatre Piece Which Utilizes All Aspects Of The Performing Arts.

### Space Biology
The Study Of Effects Of High Altitude On Humans.

### Special
A Spectacular One-Off Television Show.

### White Sidewall Haircut
A Haircut With Hair Clipped Short On The Sides.

# New for Christmas! Twin-Cartridge fountain pen
## holds 40% more ink...yet never goes near an ink bottle

**The beautiful new** SAFARI pen and pencil are like no other writing set you ever saw before.

The SAFARI pen is a true fountain pen that loads with *two cartridges of liquid ink* . . . never from an ink bottle. It holds 40% more ink than any other fountain pen . . . yet is sleekly modern and slim.

You never run out of ink, either. The second cartridge is a spare . . . always ready right in the pen. And only Esterbrook gives you a choice of 32 points . . . replaceable in seconds at any pen counter.

And the matching SAFARI pencil is completely unique, too. You feed *two feet of lead* without reloading—simply by pressing its push-top.

People expect Esterbrook's superb new SAFARI pen and pencil set to cost $25.00 or more. Guess again! The sensible price—complete with cartridges—is just $7.75. Pen alone only $3.95.

**Two cartridges instead of one**—so you always have a spare ink supply. Loading the SAFARI is so easy and clean, too. Just drop two ink cartridges into pen . . . and you're ready to *write*. When one cartridge is used up, replace it . . . and keep the other as your spare ink supply. You can buy economical packs of 6 big cartridges at any pen counter.

## *Esterbrook*®
## SAFARI*
TWIN-CARTRIDGE FOUNTAIN PEN
### only $3.95

*student    Signature Style    bookkeeping    fine writing    shaded writing*

*TRADEMARK

# *Disasters*

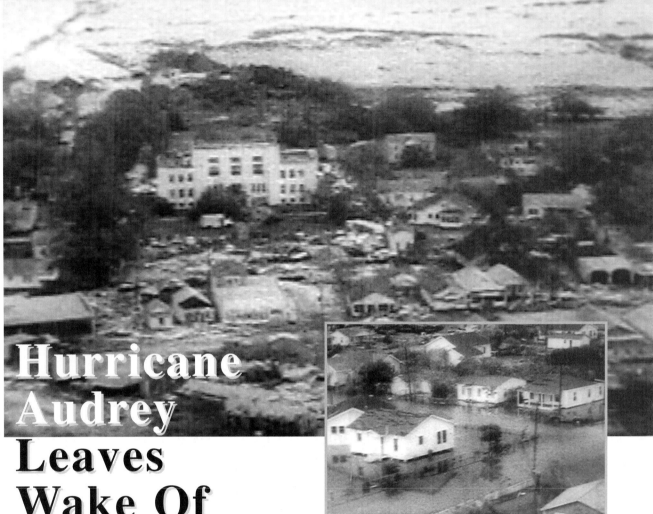

## Hurricane Audrey Leaves Wake Of Destruction In Her Path

**H**urricane Audrey roars ashore near the Texas/Louisiana border on June 27, making a shambles of towns in her path. Winds as high as 96 m.p.h. cause storm surges of up to 12 feet, extending from Galveston, TX to Cocoderie, LA.

**C**uriously, on the evening before landfall, masses of crawfish are observed fleeing the marshes in the vicinity.

# Hurricane Audrey

**A**udrey strikes without warning, leaving thousands homeless. 100,000 buildings are damaged, thousands destroyed. Cameron Parish is hardest hit, losing 90% of it's structures. Property damage is estimated at $120 million.

**O**ver 500 dead are scattered across a wide area and many days pass before the final death count can be estimated.

# BLIZZARD HITS THE MIDWEST

**H**undreds of cars are marooned as a snowstorm blankets the south and midwest with drifts of up to 30 feet in some places and a death toll of 38 persons.

**K**ansas is among the hardest hit of the five states.

**T**his transcontinental train is completely buried with more than 200 passengers marooned for over 48 hours.

**T**he last of the snow is finally removed from the train.

# NUCLEAR FALL-OUT

Radioactive Material Spreads Throughout The Countryside As Fire Breaks Out In The Windscale Pile Nuclear Reactor North Of Liverpool, England.

Kasli, USSR Is The Site Of A Chemical Explosion In Tanks Containing Nuclear Waste, Spewing Radioactive Material And Forcing The Evacuation Of The Area.

# 250 DIE IN RAIL DISASTER IN WEST PAKISTAN.

*Fire Rages Through Home For The Aged In Warrenton, Missouri Killing 72 People.*

**S**oviet Ship Eshghabad Runs Aground In The Caspian Sea, Killing 270.

**N**ortheast Airline's Flight #823 Crashes Less Than One Minute After Take-Off From New York's La Guardia Field, Killing 20 And Injuring 50.

Tornado Tears Through Kansas And Missouri Killing 48.

**July:** An Earthquake Hits Northern Iran, Killing 2,500.

**December:** An Earthquake Hits Western Iran, Killing 2,000.

San Francisco Is Hit By Its Worst Earthquake Since 1906.

# What's New

**Laika**, *a stray terrier from the streets of Moscow, becomes the first earthling in space when she is launched into earth orbit aboard the Soviet spacecraft, Sputnik 2. Outfitted with a harness and placed in a padded enclosure allowing sufficient room to stand or lie, she is supplied with automatically dispensed food and water and monitored via a television camera. No provision is made for Laika's safe return and it is believed she perished after two days instead of the planned ten, due to high temperatures in the pressurized cabin.*

# New Products & Inventions

**E**veryday consumer products have been given a new French twist, such as this stove in the shape of a snail.

**A** woman with her son leans over to remove the cover from what looks like a swan.

**G**uess again. It's a wash basin.

**A**nd finally, two products that no French household should be without... knives with boots (left), and a cigarette holder with a tiny paper umbrella to keep the smoke out of your eyes.

*The sphere above is a "core" for one kind of research atomic reactor. The metal tubes in the foreground and at the right show various test designs for holding the small uranium fuel pellets in other kinds of atomic reactors.*

# Strange new "tools" of atomic-electric power

These are some of the strange new "tools" used to produce, test, or experiment with atomic-electric power. They are among the things that will help bring electricity from the atom.

"Tools" like these are being used in developing several atomic-electric plants now under way. A number of electric light and power companies from many parts of the country are working with each other and with equipment manufacturers and the Atomic Energy Commission to develop the plants.

For more than 75 years, America's independent electric light and power companies have supplied more and more electricity to this growing nation. Today they produce more than any other single nation in the world. And they have helped develop ways to produce it more efficiently year after year. That's why you can expect electric companies to continue to do their part to advance the new science of producing electricity from the atom.

## America's Independent Electric Light and Power Companies*

*Company names on request through this magazine

The Toy Chest

THE HAMILTON WATCH COMPANY INTRODUCES THE FIRST COMMERCIAL ELECTRIC BATTERY-POWERED WRISTWATCH: THE *PACER*.

A Copenhagen Yoga Instructor Designs Earth Shoes.

## POCKET-SIZE RESUSCITATOR DEVELOPED FOR MEDICAL EMERGENCIES.

**Earl Bakken Of Medtronics, Inc., A Minneapolis Based Company, Develops The First External, Battery-Powered Cardiac Pacemaker.**

*The Delco Radio Division Of General Motors Develops All-Transistor Car Radio.*

**First U.S.-Developed Giant Weather Balloon Launched From Japan Carries Equipment To Broadcast Temperature And Pressure Readings.**

First Interstate Facsimile Communications Network To Serve Business Is Installed For Reynolds Metals Company.

First Ticket Facsimile System Installed At New York's Pennsylvania Station Allowing Customers To View Available Fares And Seating For Up To 16 Weeks Ahead On Giant Closed-Circuit TV Screens.

Curbside Banking Service Installed In Pontiac, Michigan Bank.

*Automatic Air-Traffic Control System Developed By Thomas M. Ferrill, Jr., Of Garden City, New York.*

The General Dynamics Corp. Develops First Electronic Telephone.

Johnson's Wax Corp. Introduces Glade, A Home Air Freshener That Destroys Odors Instead Of Just Masking Them.

A Water Repellent For Leather Shoes Is Developed By Knomark Company Of Brooklyn, New York Which Is Said To Protect Shoes From Rain For As Long As Six Months.

The First Portable Icebox Is Invented Using Dry Ice As The Refrigerant.

Magnetic Stud Finder Introduced By Dresden Manufacturing Of Long Beach, California.

Using The Principles Of The Ball Point Pen, The Glu-Pen Corp. Of Hampton, Virginia Introduces The First Glue Pen Which Dispenses A Small Amount Of Glue When Pressure Is Applied To The Point.

Shatterproof Plastic Window Developed by Seiberling Rubber Co. of Akron Ohio.

Flashing Runway Lights Ordered Installed at Airports by C.A.A.

A Miniature Nuclear-Powered Battery with A 5-Year Life Developed Jointly by Elgin National Watch Co. and Walter Kidde Nuclear Laboratories.

**B.F. GOODRICH CO. USES ATOMIC ENERGY FOR THE FIRST TIME TO VULCANIZE AUTOMOBILE TIRES.**

**Hot Dog Fork Designed To Roast Six Hot Dogs At A Time Introduced By Lockey Products, Chicago, Illinois.**

**Shatterproof, Washable, Chip Proof Lampshades Available For The First Time.**

**House Of Vision Reports Development Of Unbreakable Lenses For Plastic Eyeglasses That Are Almost As Scratch Proof As Glass.**

# GENERAL MOTORS

*The GM Golden Anniversary Chevrolet*

*The GM Golden Anniversary Pontiac*

*The GM Golden Anniversary Oldsmobile*

# GOLDEN FIVE for '58

Presented here are five typical offerings of 1958 automobiles from our five car Divisions in celebration of the fiftieth year of General Motors.

They are automobiles that—to be worthy of this event—were dedicated to surpass their own traditions.

And, while each maintains its own personality, all five cars benefit — as does the public — from the combined ingenuity of their own engineering staffs and the styling, research, development and testing resources of General Motors.

From the General Motors Technical Center comes a steady flow of advanced engineering and design developments—basic betterments in transmissions and engines—new ideas in comfort and safety features—new concepts in styling and appointments.

It is this General Motors leadership which has created such outstanding values in the cars now ready for your inspection in the showrooms of GM dealers.

They offer you, we believe, the widest selection and the most satisfying motoring to be found today.

*The GM Golden Anniversary Buick*

*The GM Golden Anniversary Cadillac*

**FROM THE PROGRESS OF THE PAST ... THE PROMISE OF THE FUTURE**

Pocket-Sized Television Camera Developed By Radio Corporation Of American For Military Use.

The "Legumex," A European Automatic Vegetable Peeler, Makes Its Way Into The American Market.

General Electric Company Goes Into Limited Production With Battery-Operated New Cordless Electric Clock.

Sapolin Paints, Inc., Introduces New Quick-Drying Paint.

 Albuquerque, New Mexico Is The Site Of The First Office Building To Be Successfully Solar-Heated.

First Solar Clock Developed By The General Time Corp., Of New York.

The First Sterling Silver-Tipped Ballpoint Pen Introduced By W.A. Sheaffer Co.

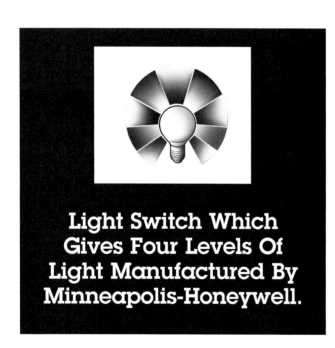

**Light Switch Which Gives Four Levels Of Light Manufactured By Minneapolis-Honeywell.**

GENERAL ELECTRIC CO. RECEIVES PATENT RIGHTS TO TOASTERS WITH ADJUSTABLE SLOTS TO ACCOMMODATE A GREATER RANGE OF SIZES.

**New Curb-Side Telephones With Plastic Hoods To Protect The Equipment Is Being Tested By The Bell Telephone Laboratories.**

LEVER BROTHERS INTRODUCES THE FIRST CONTOURED BAR OF SOAP.

LEVER BROTHERS ASSIGNED RIGHTS TO PATENT FOR SYNTHETIC PROTEIN COMPOUND MADE FROM SOYBEANS OR PEANUTS FOR USE IN MEATLESS FOOD PRODUCTS SUCH AS HAMBURGERS AND LUNCHEON MEAT.

## THE NEW "GENIE-LIFT-A-DOR," A RADIO-CONTROLLED GARAGE DOOR OPENER, IS DEVELOPED BY THE ALLIANCE MANUFACTURING COMPANY IN ALLIANCE, OHIO.

## RALSTON PURINA INTRODUCES PURINA DOG CHOW.

## THE "AEROCAR," AN AUTOMOBILE WITH COLLAPSIBLE WINGS THAT TURNS INTO A 2-PASSENGER PLANE WITH A CRUISING SPEED OF 100 M.P.H. IS DEVELOPED BY AN AMERICAN MANUFACTURER.

Zenith Radio Corp. Develops Streamlined Antenna The Size Of A Box Of Kitchen Matches.

Manhattan's Bohn Duplicator Corp. Develops A 6-Lb. Calculator That Adds, Subtracts, Divides And Multiplies Up To Ten Digits Which Will Sell For $125.

**Brooklyn Businessman Benjamin Eisendstadt Develops *Sweet 'N' Low* With His Son Marty, A Chemist.**

## Hoover Develops A Spin Dryer For Home Use.

## The Frisbee And The Hula Hoop Are Introduced By Wham-O Manufacturing.

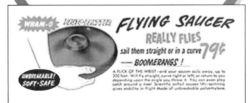

# "Any cereal starts the day right ... as long as it's Post Bran Flakes"

**LIFE IS SWELL WHEN YOU KEEP WELL** ... like you do
when you enjoy the "keep regular" benefits of Post 40% Bran Flakes.
Tastes so good, too—lots of folks eat it for the flavor alone.
That's probably why Post is the biggest-selling bran flakes in the world.
Try some—see if you don't feel swell yourself!

"ALL POST CEREALS HAPPEN TO BE JUST A LITTLE BIT BETTER"

**40% BRAN FLAKES**

*Post*

The Breakfast Foods of General Foods

# SCIENCE & MEDICINE

**I**nternational Geophysical Year Opens With Scientists And Technicians Representing 70 Nations That Will Participate In An 18-Month Environmental Study.

**U.S.** Air Force Major David G. Simons Completes Record Ascent Of 19 Miles In Pressurized Balloon.

First U. S. Nuclear Power Reactor Dedicated By Army Secretary Wilbur Brucker At Ft. Belvoir, Virginia.

First European Particle Accelerator Opens in Geneva.

Micro Computers Made Possible Through New Cryotron Device.

University Of California's Pioneering Nuclear Physicist **Ernest Orlando Lawrence** Receives $50,000 Prize From Atomic Energy Commission For His Work In Exploring The Atom.

**Largest Radio Telescope In The World Built At Jodrell Bank, England.**

Prehistoric Skull Estimated To Be About 45,000 Years Old Discovered In Cave In Iraq.

**LEADING GERMAN PHYSICISTS ABANDON ALL NUCLEAR-WEAPON RELATED RESEARCH.**

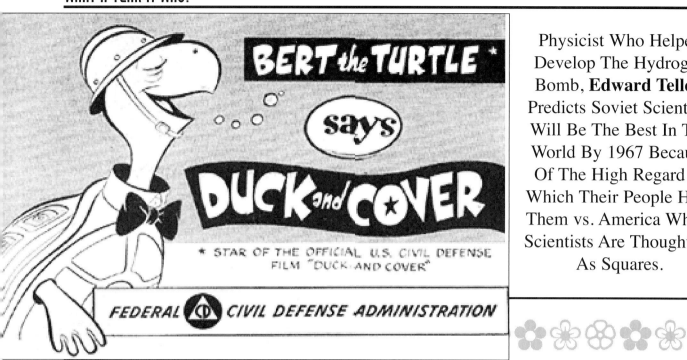

Physicist Who Helped Develop The Hydrogen Bomb, **Edward Teller**, Predicts Soviet Scientists Will Be The Best In The World By 1967 Because Of The High Regard In Which Their People Hold Them vs. America Where Scientists Are Thought Of As Squares.

The Journal Of The American Medical Association Reports That Urban Dwellers Are Safer From Atomic Fall-Out Than Folks Who Live In The Country.

# THE HEART OF THE MATTER

Physicians At Philadelphia General Hospital Develop A Tiny Microphone Enabling Scientists To Study Heart Sounds And Murmurs.

New Instrument Called The Cardioscope Allows Inside View Of The Heart.

## THE FLOWERS THAT BLOOM IN THE SPRING
(New Varieties)

### CLIMBING QUEEN ELIZABETH:
Rose and Pale Pink Double Blossom Climbing Grandiflora.

### JUNE BRIDE:
Creamy White Double Flowers With Moderate Fragrance.

### GOLD CUP (Coupe d'Or)
Deep Golden Yellow Double Flowers With Moderate Fragrance.

Loyola University Announces Development Of New Powder Food Supplement Which Provides Daily Requirement Of Nutrients.

## MASSACHUSETTS INSTITUTE OF TECHNOLOGY ANNOUNCES DEVELOPMENT OF A SYNTHETIC PENICILLIN MADE FROM FERMENTED MOLDS.

IBM makes the FORTRAN scientific programming language available to customers. It becomes the most widely used computer language for technical work.

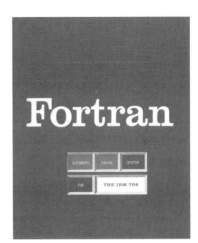

RCA Builds The World's Largest Electronic Brain For The Army Ordnance Corps. Capable Of Keeping Track Of The Army's Huge Inventory Of Up To 100 Million Facts About Tank And Automotive Spare Parts Throughout The World.

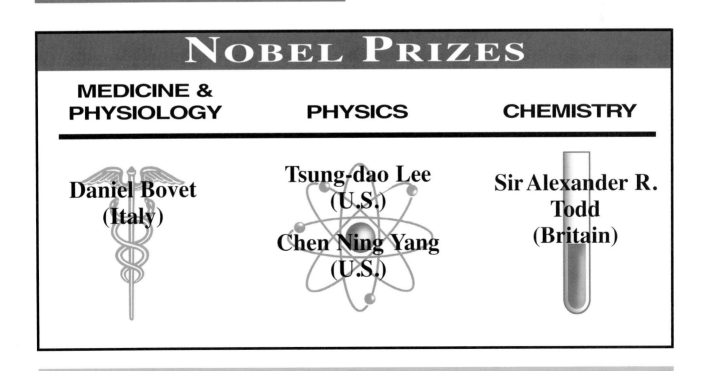

# NOBEL PRIZES

| MEDICINE & PHYSIOLOGY | PHYSICS | CHEMISTRY |
|---|---|---|
| Daniel Bovet (Italy) | Tsung-dao Lee (U.S.) Chen Ning Yang (U.S.) | Sir Alexander R. Todd (Britain) |

# The Space Race Heats Up As America Tries To Catch Up With The Soviets

America is shocked by the success of the Soviet space program, which includes launching tiny dog *Laika* into space aboard Sputnik 2.

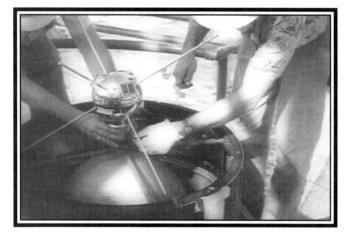

The U.S. tries to catch up by attempting to launch a grapefruit size satellite on the Vanguard rocket.

The results are disastrous as the rocket blows up two seconds after firing from its Cocoa Beach, Florida launching site.

# Eisenhower Goes To Paris To Discuss Soviet Space Supremacy

In the shadow of Sputnik, President Eisenhower goes to Paris to meet with NATO leaders to discuss the Soviet threat. A decision is reached that three European nations will be armed with intermediate range missiles.

President Eisenhower is greeted warmly by the French people.

While in meetings, Eisenhower receives word of the successful launching of the Atlas Intercontinental Ballistic Missile on a 500-mile flight from Cape Canaveral, which puts America in a position of beginning to challenge Russia's space supremacy.

A watch spring implanted in her heart keeps a Detroit woman alive.

At the Cleveland Clinic, Dr. Willem Kolff implants the first totally artificial heart in the chest of an animal.

Dr. George Pincus Of The Worcester Institute Of Experimental Biology Develops Pill For Prevention Of Pregnancy In Humans

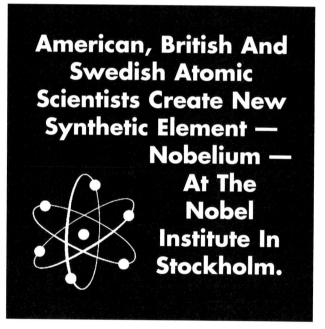

**American, British And Swedish Atomic Scientists Create New Synthetic Element — Nobelium — At The Nobel Institute In Stockholm.**

**Stanford Medical School Successfully Treats Cancerous Tumors With Their 6-Million Volt Linear Accelerator.**

*Columbia University Scientists Discover Mountain Range Rising 5,000 Feet Above The Ocean Floor On The Arctic Ice Pack Drifting Toward The North Pole.*

# MEDICINE

## Surgeons Find That In Cases Of Uncomplicated Procedures, Patients Recover More Quickly At Home.

## Breathing Is More Difficult For Premature Infants Who Are Placed On Their Stomachs Vs. Their Backs.

American Medical Association Releases Report From American Cancer Society Revealing A Strong Connection Between Cigarette Smoking and Deaths From Lung Cancer.

U.S. Public Health Service Takes Official Anti-Smoking Position Because Of Increasing Evidence Of The Link Between Cigarette Smoking And Lung Cancer.

## Poetry Used Successfully As A Healing Aid In Philadelphia State Hospital.

❑ American Medical Association to study use of stimulants by athletes.

❑ Johns Hopkins University announces development of a vaccine against major common cold virus developed by Winston H. Price.

❑ National Association of Chiropodists renamed American Podiatry Association.

❑ Air Force veterinarian Harry A. Gorman's all-metal device to replace hip joint in injured dogs used on human victim of rheumatoid arthritis.

❑ Canadian psychiatrist names new neurosis: *Audiophilia:* excessive passion for hi-fi sound and equipment.

- **Sedative Drug Thalidomide Released In Europe And Canada Widely Used To Counter Morning Sickness In Pregnant Women.**

- **Orinase, First Oral Medication For Diabetes, Introduced By Upjohn.**

## HERE'S SOMETHING TO CHEW ON

According To A Report Released By Seton Hall College, There Is A Definite Link Between Personality And Tooth Decay. A Person Inclined To Have Bad Teeth Has Characteristics Something Like These:

- **Independent Self Starters**
- **Welcomes Responsibility**
- **Interested In Intellectual Pursuits**

According To A Study Conducted By New York's Yeshiva University, Men On Skid Row Are Just As Intelligent As Their Non-Skid Row Counterparts.

**Surgeons Enter The Coronary Arteries For The First Time And Remove Fatty Clots That Lead To Heart Attacks.**

Medical Investigators Report In The Journal Of The American Medical Association That Eating Red Meat Before A Football Game Does Not Improve A Player's Performance And That Athletes Live Just As Long As Non-Athletes.

**Doctors Warn That A Husband Should Never Donate Blood To His Wife Because Of The Danger Of RH-Factor Incompatibility.**

## OH MY ACHING HEAD

According To A Study On Headaches Released By Louisiana State Hospital, Recurring Headaches Are Most Prevalent In Single Women Under 20 And People Who Are Divorced Or Separated Are More Likely To Have Them Than Their Married Counterparts.

Photographed at the Blind Brook Polo Club, Purchase, N. Y.

## THE SPORTS-CAR OF SPORTSMEN

*Especially* engineered to be driven by the man who lives for swift, sure-footed action in its fullest measure . . . *deliberately* styled to make him the envy of everyone else. Make a date for a test-drive today!

*Austin-Healey*
100-SIX

A product of The British Motor Corporation, Ltd., makers of Austin-Healey, Austin, MG, Magnette, Morris and Riley cars
**Represented in the United States by**
**hambro** AUTOMOTIVE CORPORATION • 27 West 57th Street, New York 19, N.Y.
Sold and serviced by a nationwide network of distributors and dealers.

## PROFILE OF THE JAYWALKER

- **Potential Suicides**
- **Immature**
- **Personality Deviates**
- **Unconsciously Seeking Danger**
- **Or...Maybe Just In A Hurry To Get Somewhere**

---

- Hypnosis Found To Be An Effective Anesthetic During An Operation.
- World Health Organization Develops New Technique For Rabies Protection By Giving Small Doses Of Vaccine To Potential Victims.

---

According To Psychology Professor Dr. Cleo Dawson Women Expect To Be Bossed And Are More Comfortable In That Role Than In The Role Of Being Bossy.

The Nobel Institute In Sweden Develops Blood Test That Could Determine If A Person Is Mentally Ill.

Use Of Forceps To Aid Delivery Thought To Be Responsible For 70% Of Cerebral Palsy Cases — Cesarean Section Seen As A Safer Alternative.

Chronically Depressed Mental Patients Stay That Way Because Of Their Failure To See Anything Happy In Their Future.

The Journal Of The American Medical Association Publishes A Report Stating That Tranquilizers Can Be Injurious To Mental Health And Can Cause Serious Toxic Reactions.

---

## ① #1 KILLER DISEASE IN THE UNITED STATES: HEART DISEASE.

---

### WELL, I DON'T MIND IF I DO, SWEETIE, FOR MEDICINAL PURPOSES ONLY, OF COURSE!

A Doctor At New York's St. Luke's Hospital Recommends Moderate Use Of Alcohol By Older Persons As An Excellent Way Of Improving The Health Of Their Mind And Body.

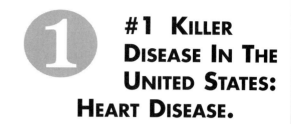

---

THE CHEMICAL COMPOSITION OF TEARS THOUGHT TO BE ABLE TO DETERMINE THE STATE OF A PERSON'S HEALTH.

---

According To A Study Done At The University Of Wisconsin, Waking Up Tired Morning After Morning Could Indicate That You Are Anxious, Tense, Disinterested, Bored Or Frustrated In Reaching Your Life's Goals And Are Unwilling To Face Your Everyday Problems.

**Larger, Frequent Feedings Said To Ward Off Colic In Breast-Fed Babies.**

## YOU ARE WHAT YOU EAT PERSONALITY PROFILE

| | |
|---|---|
| **Finicky** | *Active & Impulsive* |
| **Vegetable Lovers** | *Work Alone On Theoretical Problems; Better Planner Than Administrator.* |
| **Salad Lovers** | *Outgoing, Social* |
| **Starch Lovers** | *Teamworker; Deals With Day To Day Problems; Good Administrator.* |

- Two Philadelphia Surgeons Drs. Warren S. Reeses And Turgut N. Hamdi Successfully Implant Artificial Lens Following Cataract Operation.
- Baby Pacifiers Win Favor With Doctors Once Again As A Means Of Preventing Prolonged Thumbsucking And Dental Disfigurement.

## BUT HONEY, BE REASONABLE, WHERE AM I GOING TO FIND COAL AT THIS TIME OF NIGHT — HOW ABOUT A PICKLE?

*According To A Nutrition Survey Done Of Pregnant Women, 187 Out Of 1,000 Crave Coal, While One Wanted To Eat The Plaster Off Of Her Wall.*

## PUT DOWN THAT HAMBURGER & FRENCH FRIES

The Trend Toward Giving Solid Foods To Infants Is Wrong According To A Pediatrician Who Believes Solids Should Be Introduced Around The Same Time As The Baby Gets Its First Teeth.

- Darvon Is Introduced As A Pain Killer.
- One-Minute Test For Syphilis Is Developed.

The Average Age Of Lung Cancer Victims Is Around 61.

Smokers Are More Likely To Give Birth Prematurely.

A Study Of 100 Heart Attack Victims Under Age 40 Reveals Stress The Primary Trigger.

## A PIECE OF CHOCOLATE CAKE TO KEEP YOU WARM AT NIGHT

Soldiers Fed A Snack Of Between 600 and 1,200 Calories Before Going To Sleep In Sub-Zero Temperatures Woke Up Fewer Times Throughout The Night And Had Less Discomfort From The Cold Than Those Soldiers Who Did Not Have A Snack. Who's Got The Pizza?

## *PASSINGS*

**Admiral Richard Byrd, U.S. Explorer First To Fly Over North And South Poles, Dies At 69.**

**Joseph William Kennedy, One Of The Discoverers Of Plutonium, The Essential Element Of The Atomic Bomb, Dies At 40.**

# So right for all the family—BLUE BELL clothes

You get so much for so little! Good looks, long wear—completely washable, sizes for everyone—98¢ to $4.98

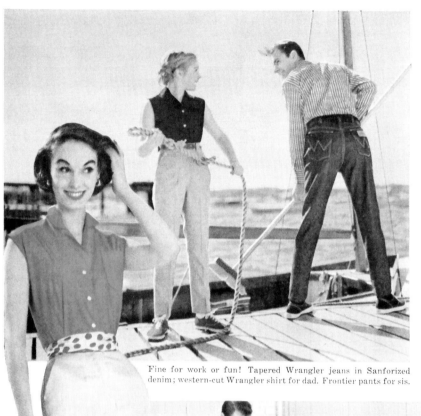

Fine for work or fun! Tapered Wrangler jeans in Sanforized denim; western-cut Wrangler shirt for dad. Frontier pants for sis.

Authentic western-cut Blue Bell Wrangler jeans, shirts, preferred by rodeo champions like Jim Shoulders. Sizes for all.

Trim Blue Bell Jeanie pedal pushers and blouse for all the girls

On the job or off! Blue Bell matching shirts, pants keep their neat looks long. Sanforized cotton twills; sizes for dad and son.

Blue Bell Jeanie shorts, blouses for mom, sis, too.

Look for this Blue Bell emblem—it's your unconditional guarantee of satisfaction

Blue Bell, Inc., Empire State Bldg., New York 1, N. Y.—Canada, W. Howick Mfg. Co., Montreal

124

# It's a Living

## ANNUAL SALARIES

| | |
|---|---|
| Accountants | $ 6,000 |
| Airline Pilots | $ 13,000 |
| Financial Executives | $ 11,300 |
| Dentists | $ 12,300 |
| Lawyers | $ 10,200 |
| Motion Picture Performer | $ 25,000 |
| Physicians | $ 14,718 |
| Psychologists | $ 8,000 |
| Surgeons | $ 18,975 |
| Teachers (High School & Elementary) | $ 5,000 |
| Television Producers | $ 30,000 |
| Television Performers | $ 10,000 |

**Average Hourly Pay:**
**$ 2.10**

**The Federal Hourly**
**Minimum Wage:**
**$ 1.00**

**Per Capita**
**Personal Income:**
**$ 2,050**

*Illustrated above left to right: #6597 paper-wrapped, #6587 disc, #1207 woodcased.*

## Corrections are a snap with JOB-MATED ERASERS*

It's natural to make mistakes whether typing, drawing, writing with pencil or ink . . . on letterheads, carbon tissues, vellums or literally hundreds of kinds of paper.

Now, once and for all, you can forget those human errors. *Change your mind as often as you like.* Because Eberhard Faber makes a job-mated eraser° for every purpose and every paper. Try one today—at better stores everywhere.

SINCE 1849 **EBERHARD FABER** WILKES-BARRE, PA. TORONTO

Erasers Easily Eliminate Errors

°*Mated to the paper type and designed for the erasure job*

Trademarks Reg. U. S. Pat. Off.

Pink Pearl "100" . . . Rubkleen "6002" . . . Ruby "112" . . . Star Plastic Cleaner . . . Specify choice of eraser on your company letterhead for free sample

# AMERICA'S FIRST COMMERCIAL JET TAKES TO THE SKIES

The first commercial jet transport, a giant Boeing Stratoliner, gets ready to make its maiden flight from Seattle.

The transport is about to go into 12 months of rigorous flight testing to qualify for a civil aeronautics administration flight certificate. If it passes all the tests, a fleet of 150 of these planes, already in production, will go into service.

## DIGITAL Equipment Corporation Is Founded

### PASSINGS

Diamond king **SIR ERNEST OPPENHEIMER**, owner of the De Beers Mines and controller of 95% of the world's diamond products, dies at age 77 in Johannesburg.

Automobile pioneer **LOUIS SEMPLE CLARKE**, who built his first car in 1896, dies at age 90.

*Proctor & Gamble Acquire Charmin Paper Mills And Clorox*

# THE PRICE THAT WAS

| | |
|---|---|
| Baseball | 2.77 |
| Bath Towel | .74 |
| Coca-Cola | .05 |
| Iron, Electric | .27 |
| Flashlight Battery | .14 |
| Diapers, Fleece | 2.69 |

| | |
|---|---|
| Aspirin (100 ct.) | $ .49 |
| Baby Powder (4 oz.) | .49 |
| Bath Salts | 2.50 |
| Billfold, Ladies | 5.00 |
| Blistex Lip Medication | .39 |
| Box Spring | 49.50 |
| Candelabra, Sterling Silver | .155.00 |
| Candy (Lifesavers) | .05 |

| | |
|---|---|
| China, Cup & Saucer Set | $3.50 |
| Cigarette Lighter | .17 |
| Cigar | .10 |
| Clearasil Acne Medication | .69 |
| Clothes Dryer | 199.95 |
| Cold Medicine | 1.00 |
| Cologne & Dusting Powder Set | 3.00 |
| Cooking Pot & Cover, Stainless Steel (2 pcs.) | 5.99 |
| Cough Syrup | .39 |
| Curtains & Valance | .97 |
| Dental Cream | .65 |
| Deodorant (Cream) | .43 |
| Electric Shaver | 14.95 |
| Ex-Lax Laxative | .79 |
| Eye Shadow Stick | 1.00 |

| | |
|---|---|
| Eyebrow Pencil, Automatic | $ .79 |
| Eyelash Curler | 1.00 |
| Hair Tonic | .49 |
| Home Permanent, Toni | 2.29 |
| Lamps, Boudoir | 1.47 |
| Lighter Fuel (8 oz.) | .49 |
| Lipstick | 1.10 |
| LIFE Magazine | .25 |
| LIFE Magazine, 1-yr subscription | 6.75 |
| Make-Up (Liquid) | 1.50 |
| Mascara | 1.25 |
| Mattress | 49.50 |
| Mixed Nuts | 2.00 |
| Nail Polish | .75 |
| Pan, Frying (Electric) | 22.95 |
| Percolator (Automatic) | 16.95 |
| Rain Boots | 2.00 |

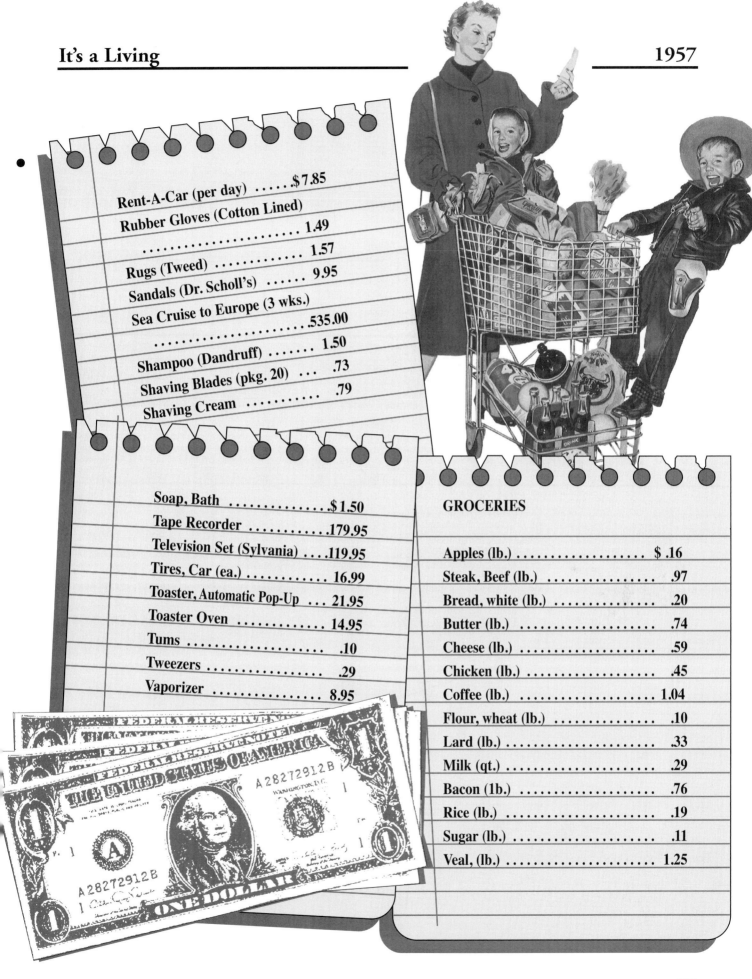

| | |
|---|---|
| Rent-A-Car (per day) | $7.85 |
| Rubber Gloves (Cotton Lined) | 1.49 |
| Rugs (Tweed) | 1.57 |
| Sandals (Dr. Scholl's) | 9.95 |
| Sea Cruise to Europe (3 wks.) | 535.00 |
| Shampoo (Dandruff) | 1.50 |
| Shaving Blades (pkg. 20) | .73 |
| Shaving Cream | .79 |

| | |
|---|---|
| Soap, Bath | $1.50 |
| Tape Recorder | 179.95 |
| Television Set (Sylvania) | 119.95 |
| Tires, Car (ea.) | 16.99 |
| Toaster, Automatic Pop-Up | 21.95 |
| Toaster Oven | 14.95 |
| Tums | .10 |
| Tweezers | .29 |
| Vaporizer | 8.95 |

**GROCERIES**

| | |
|---|---|
| Apples (lb.) | $ .16 |
| Steak, Beef (lb.) | .97 |
| Bread, white (lb.) | .20 |
| Butter (lb.) | .74 |
| Cheese (lb.) | .59 |
| Chicken (lb.) | .45 |
| Coffee (lb.) | 1.04 |
| Flour, wheat (lb.) | .10 |
| Lard (lb.) | .33 |
| Milk (qt.) | .29 |
| Bacon (1b.) | .76 |
| Rice (lb.) | .19 |
| Sugar (lb.) | .11 |
| Veal, (lb.) | 1.25 |

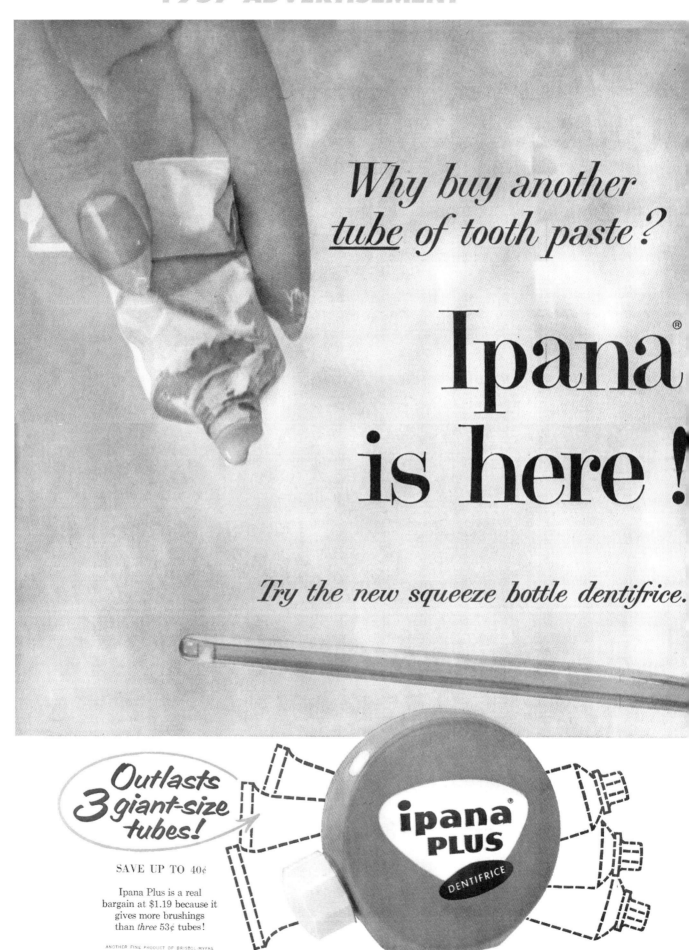

Why buy another *tube* of tooth paste?

# Ipana® is here!

*Try the new squeeze bottle dentifrice.*

*Outlasts* **3** *giant-size tubes!*

SAVE UP TO 40¢

Ipana Plus is a real bargain at $1.19 because it gives more brushings than *three* 53¢ tubes!

ANOTHER FINE PRODUCT OF BRISTOL-MYERS

ipana® PLUS DENTIFRICE

ACTUAL SIZE: Fits easily on any bathroom shelf!

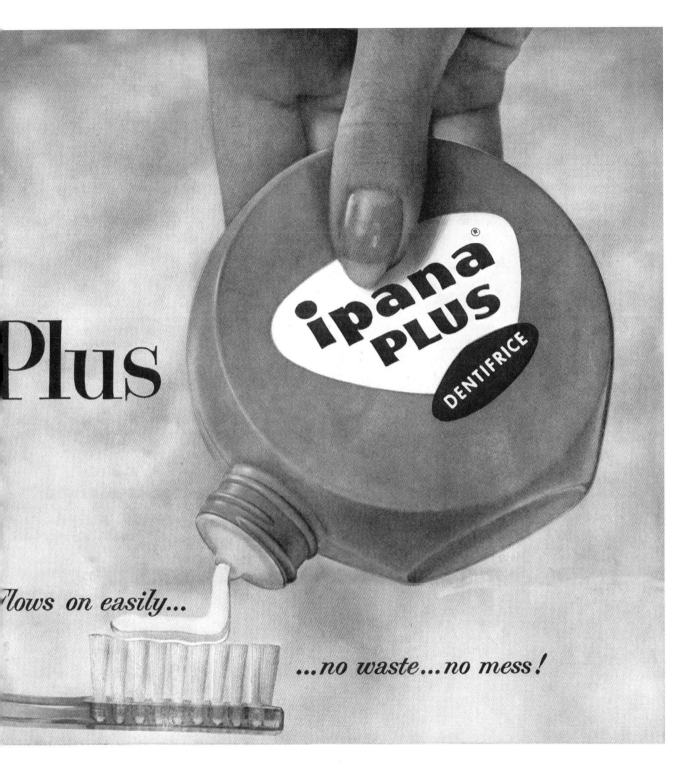

Plus

Flows on easily...

...no waste...no mess!

## New flowing formula leaves teeth feeling cleaner, whole mouth fresher than tooth paste!*

Just *looking* at it, you know you're going to like it—this wonderful new way to brush your teeth. Once you *use* new Ipana Plus...well, you'll just never go back to your tooth paste tube again!

New Ipana Plus is so much *easier* to use. A gentle squeeze, and just the right amount flows onto your brush. Stop squeezing, it stops flowing. No waste or mess ever. Unbreakable plastic bottle keeps its neat, new look from the very first squeeze to the last.

New flowing formula is ready to go to work quicker than any tooth paste. It penetrates tiny, hidden crevices between teeth. *Most people who tested it—even against their favorite paste—said Ipana Plus left their teeth feeling cleaner, their whole mouth more refreshed. (With kids who tried it, it was love at first taste!)

Start brushing with new Ipana Plus today. Until you do, you'll just never know how clean your teeth and mouth can feel!

131

## WOMEN'S CLOTHES & LINGERIE

| | |
|---|---:|
| Bra | $ 2.50 |
| Briefs (4) | .97 |
| Dress, Evening | 16.50 |
| High Heels | 9.95-13.95 |
| Nightgown | 6.00 |
| Nylons (pair) | .87 |
| Pajamas (silk) | 30.00 |
| Scarves (silk & rayon) | .77 |
| Slip (full) | 9.00 |
| Slippers | 7.95 |

## MEN'S CLOTHES

| | |
|---|---:|
| Belt | $ 5.00 |
| Cuff Links (black onyx) | 13.50 |
| Hat | 5.95 |
| Jacket (nylon) | 5.95 |
| Socks | 1.00 |
| Thermal T-Shirt | 1.50 |

### PAN AMERICAN AIRLINES
**See The World On The World-Wide Plan**

| Typical Round Trips | Minimum Down Payment | 20 Monthly Payments |
|---|---|---|
| Miami-Havana or Nassau | $ 4 | $ 6 |
| Houston-Mexico City | 8 | 6 |
| New York-Bermuda | 10 | 5 |
| West Coast Cities-Hawaii | 25 | 13 |
| Boston-Shannon | 37 | 20 |
| New York-Rome | 55 | 30 |
| Around The World | 135 | 70 |

### LONG DISTANCE RATES ARE LOW
**Daytime Station-to-Station Calls**

| For Example: | First 3 Minutes | Each Added Minute |
|---|---|---|
| Augusta, GA. to Charlotte, N.C. | 65¢ | 20¢ |
| Chicago to Indianapolis | 70¢ | 20¢ |
| Baltimore to Boston | $1.10 | 30¢ |
| Los Angeles to New York | $2.50 | 65¢ |

Rates are lower after 6 pm and all day Sunday. Add 10% federal excise tax.

## MACY'S NEW YORK RECORDS $2 MILLION IN SALES IN ONE DAY, THE HIGHEST EVER RECORDED FOR A DEPARTMENT STORE.

Eli Broad And Donald Kaufman Form Building Company Parlaying Their First Investment Of $25,000 Into Sales of $250,000 On The First Week-End Of Business.

J. Willard Marriott, Owner Of Washington D.C.'s Famous Hot Shoppes, Builds One Of The World's Largest Motels, The Twin Bridges Marriott Motor Hotel, On Seven Acres Along The Potomac In Arlington, Virginia.

The Fiat, An Italian Manufactured Automobile, Enters The U.S. Market.

After Three Years And $250 Million In Research And Development, Ford Unveils Its Latest Model—*The Edsel*.

The British Introduce "The Frisky," A Miniature Car With A Gear Shift Similar To A Motorcycle And The Capability Of Getting 90 Miles To A Gallon Of Gas.

The First Toyota Car Arrives In The United States.

Volkswagen Sells 200,000 Beetles.

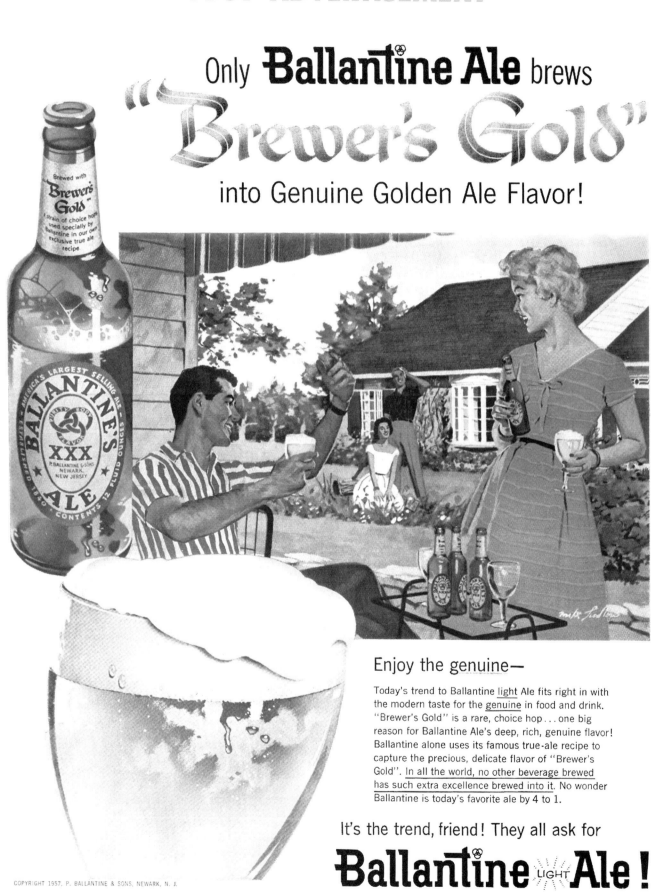

Only **Ballantine Ale** brews
"Brewer's Gold"
into Genuine Golden Ale Flavor!

### Enjoy the genuine—

Today's trend to Ballantine light Ale fits right in with the modern taste for the genuine in food and drink. "Brewer's Gold" is a rare, choice hop...one big reason for Ballantine Ale's deep, rich, genuine flavor! Ballantine alone uses its famous true-ale recipe to capture the precious, delicate flavor of "Brewer's Gold". In all the world, no other beverage brewed has such extra excellence brewed into it. No wonder Ballantine is today's favorite ale by 4 to 1.

It's the trend, friend! They all ask for

**Ballantine** LIGHT **Ale** !

134

# EUROPEAN COMMON MARKET TREATY SIGNED IN ROME

Rome City Hall is the site where an historic event is about to take place.

Long a dream, the European Common Market takes its first step forward as representatives from six European nations gather to eradicate customs barriers.

German Chancellor Adenauer, one of the chief statesmen at the conference, leads the discussions.

Belgium's representative signs the treaty, the first of several which are expected to unify Western Europe economically within the next 15 years.

With abolition of tariff barriers and the industrial integration of these nations, a new chapter is opened, economically uniting former enemies.

You'll feel a very special kind of pride the day you park a new Chevrolet in your driveway. Maybe you'll even find yourself looking out the window, now and then, just for the pleasure of seeing it there. It's a beautiful sight to behold—fresh and alert, with a certain ready-to-go spirit written all over it.

And when the neighbors drop by to "look 'er over," you'll be prouder than ever. They'll see fine construction and finishing touches everywhere. They'll feel the extra solidity of Body by Fisher, and they'll see the deeper luster of Chevy's *lacquer* paint job.

Then they'll want a ride around the block to see if Chevrolet is as sweet, smooth and sassy as it looks. That's how people become happy Chevy owners. Stop by your Chevrolet dealer's and you'll see what we mean. . . . Chevrolet Division of General Motors, Detroit 2, Mich.

*More people drive Chevrolets than any other car.*

# You get more
## to be proud of in a Chevy!

*More beautifully built and shows it—the Bel Air Sport Coupe with Body by Fisher.*

FROM THE FUNSPOTS OF THE WORLD

*Phil Rose*

*Fashion*

The 1956 film And God Created Woman hits American screens. The sight of a bikini-clad **Brigitte Bardot**, heats up demands for skimpier swimsuits.

# *Fashion*

## COCO CHANEL

The accolades pour in for Chanel, now a vital 71. Neiman-Marcus honors her with its Golden Anniversary Award for her enduring fashion contributions and for her ever-popular perfume, **Chanel No. 5**. *Life* magazine's August 19 issue carries a tribute to Chanel titled "Just a Simple Little Dressmaker."

*Chanel, circa 1930*

Variations on her famous two-piece knit jersey '20s suits are still in great demand and she remains an influencial marker for the young turks of couture. A tireless innovator, she introduces her new chain-handled quilted leather handbags – an instant success!

# WHAT A YEAR IT WAS!

# FRENCH *Flair*

## BERMUDA IS THE SITE FOR THE INTRODUCTION OF FRENCH DESIGNER GIVENCHY'S NEW LINE OF SWIMWEAR.

A distinctive feature of this colorful suit *(above)* are the separate pants underneath the tubular sheath.

Two novelty suits *(left)*, one reminiscent of the '20s with its long-legged look, have been made exciting with a vibrant mosaic print and pants that can be rolled up to the more traditional length.

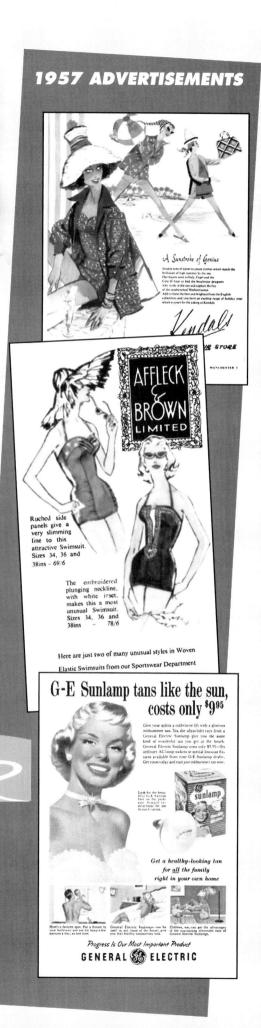
140

# Balmain
## Unveils His New Spring Line

According to French designer Pierre Balmain, *suppleness* is the word for Spring fashions using crepe, muslins and jerseys.

A sumptuous evening gown of tulle over satin, set off with a stunning diamond necklace and earring set, makes this ensemble fit for a royal wedding.

A lovely silk chiffon strapless evening gown with a vibrant floral design.

A light jersey dress falls into soft flounces.

# DESIGNERS MAKE

### BALENCIAGA

A slip dress from his winter collection has a silk chiffon under dress with yards of lace material on the outside.

**THE FRENCH |** Ten years after the dominating influence of **Dior**'s "New Look" in the fashion world, the Chemise or "The Sack" is introduced by French designers **Givenchy** and **Balenciaga**. Shaped like a giant almond with sleeves, and obscuring the silhouette, American women complain that the Sack dress is hard to iron while American men complain about the lack of sensuousness. Regardless of the objections, the Sack influences designers, even in America. So much so that in March, *Time* magazine features the undisputed giant of fashion, Dior, on its cover. The accompanying story states that Paris designers like Givenchy and and Balenciaga will change the shape of clothing everywhere.

### HUBERT GIVENCHY

Launches his Paris collection to unveil his "Sack," launching the trend for straight shift dresses which anticipate the loose and short look to come.

*Italian film director Federico Fellini is enchanted by the changes in women's clothing—especially the sack dress that eleminated women's curves. "One day," he says, "I saw women walking along dressed in a fantastic and extraordinary way, so fascinating that it set light to my imagination."*

## PASSING

### CHRISTIAN DIOR

The creator of the revolutionary "New Look," and recipient of France's Legion Of Honor decoration for breathing new life into France's fashion industry, dies at 52.

**Pierre Cardin** Unveils His First Complete Collection.

# THEIR MARK...

The black silk polka-dot dress below, with bubble skirt and soft tie at the neck, can be worn with a matching white wool cardigan.

**THE AMERICANS |** Over the objections of American women and men who feel the "Sack" dress lacks sensuality, American designers fall in step with the Parisians, though somewhat downplaying the French *shapelessness*. **Luis Estevez** combines the straightness of sack with a lavish overdress of veil material. Free-form takes over some design with the look of ballooning skirts and bubble dresses. American designers are comfortable with the silhouette in various forms: **Claire McCardell** creates a "string bean" silhouette with a dress-length cashmere pullover sweater. **Norman Norell** offers a beltless chemise and tubular tunic.

Basic sheath dress shown in black jersey (above left) and bubble skirt dress (top right).

## fashion trends fashion trends fashion trends

### for the GUYS

Styles range from the clean-scrubbed Pat Boone preppy look to beatnik chic consisting of khaki pants, sweater and sandals. Sales of blue jeans skyrocket — especially to teenagers of both genders.

### for the Girls

Light, loosely-woven fabrics with bold patterns in deep red, orange, yellow, cobalt blue and green are the most popular colors, with shades of brown competing with black for evening wear. Sharp pointed toes and medium high heels highlight fancy dress shoes.

# Stars and socialites model fashions unveiled at recent charity ball at the Palm Beach Estate of Mrs. Horace Dodge, II

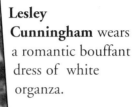

**Lesley Cunningham** wears a romantic bouffant dress of white organza.

A picture hat completes the ensemble.

A floppy hat to keep the sun off her oh-so-delicate face.

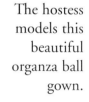

The hostess models this beautiful organza ball gown.

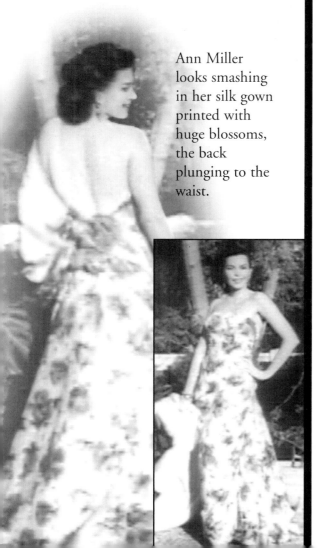

**Rita Moreno**'s strapless gown with a matching coat has a Grecian motif and is quite stunning.

Ann Miller looks smashing in her silk gown printed with huge blossoms, the back plunging to the waist.

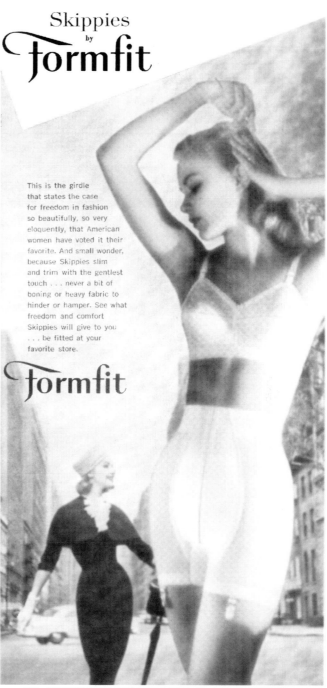

# The Three-Piece Ensemble

The look of the ultimate high fashion ensemble becomes available in various price ranges. The three-piece look offers dress-jacket combinations with slim-to-generous collars.

Moss green jersey dress with matching cropped jacket. ($69.95)

Sapphire blue tweed suit with straight-cut jacket ($47.00) shown with a matching blue silk blouse. ($10.00)

Red tweed suit with matching handbag and beret.

A bright red knitted wool suit with a printed silk blouse in shades of red and gold.

Brown and grey check suit with belted jacket.

Deep red dress with matching jacket.

Straight black tweed jacket with sable collar, slim skirt.

Basic black wool suit, slim skirt, lightly fitted jacket and off-the-neck collar.

Two-piece light pink wool crepe dress with pleated skirt and overblouse softly cinched at the waist.

Light blue silk coat worn just above the knees sweeps backward into a light flair.

# 1957 ADVERTISEMENTS

ALL NEW with light Golden

The only standard typewriter

up to 26% LESS TYPING E

STOP pound-pounding away half your strength every day!

Lightest touch in standard typewriter history... brings you easy tap-tap typing! The totally new Underwood "Touch-Master" ends back-breaking, pound-pound typing forever! Just a light tap-tap puts those Golden-Touch keys into action. Immediately you'll feel the wonderful difference!

For a Golden-Touch demonstration, call your Underwood Showroom, listed in the Yellow Pages.

Magic Ex
Extra-easy
does it!
Extra-sma
Extra-clea
Touch.
Extra-sma
Beach Beig
Underwoo

**underwood** *only standard typewriter with Golden-Touch*

Japanese Ladies" shirtwaist, skirt cut in pleats and gores, in finest cotton. Fabric and dress created by Constance Howarth, one of the world's top ten designers – and a Lancashire girl

EXCLUSIVE IN BOLTON
TO
*Dorothy Dearnaley*
FIFTY-EIGHT NEWPORT STREET, BOLTON
TELEPHONE 2009
AGENT FOR **WETHERALL** BOND STREET SPORTSCLOTHES

Shoppers!
Make **SMASHING** Savings

**10 DAYS ONLY**
Wednesday, January 9th, through Saturday, January 19th

on these eleven outstanding values

# WOOLWORTH'S
*January*
# SUPER-SALE

*Better hurry — they'll go like magic*

...and all through January — storewide savings during Woolworth's month-long

**97¢ SALE**

## SALE $1⁵⁷ EA.

### STURDY TWEED RUGS

**SAVE 41¢** Take 'em home for every room. You can't afford to miss this bargain. Cut pile tweed rugs of viscose and acetate. Latex back; fringed ends. 25″ x 37″. Gold, Aqua, Red, Green, Pink, Grey. Reg. $1.98 each.

## SALE 2 FOR 97¢

### LUXURIOUS CANNON BATH TOWELS

**SAVE 41¢** Just try to match this terrific value anywhere. Fluffy, thick bath towels 22″ x 44″ in Cannon solid pastels or smart stripes. Regularly 69¢ ea.

## SALE 97¢ COMPLETE

### CAFE CURTAINS & VALANCE

**SAVE 52¢** Brighten up the house with the newest curtain fashion at a great savings! Smooth cotton broadcloth. 50″ over-all width x 36″ length. Valance 70″ x 8″ included. Latest designs. Red, Pink, Gold. Regularly $1.49 pair.

Listen To The **WOOLWORTH HOUR**

Every Sunday afternoon Percy Faith, his Orchestra and Chorus, with outstanding guest stars, broadcasting "The Best in Music" for full hour, *live* from New York, over the CBS Radio network.

# SALE $1⁴⁷ EA.

**BEAUTIFUL 14" BOUDOIR LAMPS**

**SAVE 51¢** Amazing lamp value. Get them for every bedroom. Lamps with matching shades. White glass or gleaming brass color base. Regularly $1.98 each.

# SALE 2 FOR 97¢
Plus tax

**FABULOUS COSTUME JEWELRY**

**SAVE 21¢** Smashing value in jewelry for every occasion! Top-fashion necklaces, bracelets, earrings, brooches. Sparkling simulated jewels, rhinestones, gold color, silvery metals. These'll go fast, so don't wait! Reg. 59¢ ea.

# SALE 97¢ PR.

**DOUBLE RUFFLE DACRON CURTAINS**

**SAVE 52¢** Imagine Dacron at this low, low price! Dress up your windows with tier curtains. 60" over-all width x 36" length. Lovely fresh colors: White, Yellow, Pink or Green. Regularly $1.49 pair.

# SALE 2 FOR 77¢

**LARGE SILK AND RAYON SCARVES**

**SAVE 35%** Get armfuls! It's your chance to own imported silk scarves without paying fabulous prices. Large 33" x 33" size in exciting colors. Gay prints. Regularly 59¢ each.

# SALE 2 PR. FOR 87¢

**FIRST QUALITY NYLONS**

**SAVE 31¢** Buy a supply! Exquisite full-fashioned nylons at a next-to-nothing price. Hurry in, they'll go fast! Newest fashion shades in 51 gauge, 15 denier. Sizes 9 to 10½. Reg. 59¢ pr.

# SALE 4 FOR 97¢

**LADIES' FAVORITE BRIEFS**

**SAVE 38%** Terrific reduction. Buy dozens! Full-cut acetate briefs; popular year round. With purchase of 4 save 59¢. White only. Sizes 5, 6, 7, 8. Regularly 39¢ pair.

Remember, there's also a storewide

# 97¢ SALE

going on for the whole month of January! Watch for 97¢ specials at Woolworth's all month long! (The 11 articles shown here are on sale only from Wednesday, Jan. 9th through Saturday, Jan. 19th.)

# SALE 3 PR. FOR 87¢

**MEN'S NYLON S-T-R-E-T-C-H SOCKS**

**SAVE 28¢** Buy 'em by the dozen for every man in the house! 100% nylon ribbed socks. One size fits sizes 10 to 13. Navy Blue, Brown, Charcoal, Black or Grey. Reg. 3 pr. for $1.15.

# SALE 17¢ COMPLETE

**IMPORTED CHINA CUP AND SAUCER**

**SAVE 37%** At this low price you'll want a dozen of these beautifully delicate, expensive-looking china cups and saucers. Two shapes, three designs. Moss Rose, Violet or Columbia Rose. Reg. 27¢.

# F. W. WOOLWORTH CO.

149

# The Millinery Institute Of America Presents Its Spring Collection

An oversized straw picture hat trimmed in giant flowers.

This large sailor is covered with silk roses and stems.

A tall helmet of baby orchids trimmed with grapes and velvet leaves.

This one is made of stiff lace with black velvet ribbon running through it.

An off-the-face turban draped with a long chiffon scarf.

"Easter On Fifth Avenue" is the name of this casino circle of satin ribbon with straw braid.

# CRAZY HATS

## *for Spring from British Columbia*

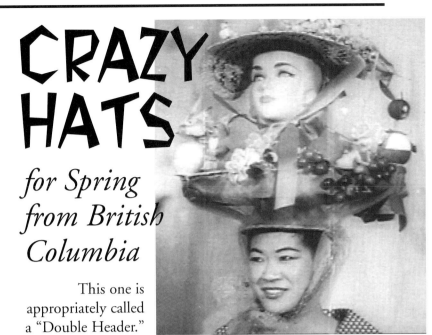

This one is appropriately called a "Double Header."

One of the models from the Chinese YWCA in Vancouver wears "the biggest hat in the world."

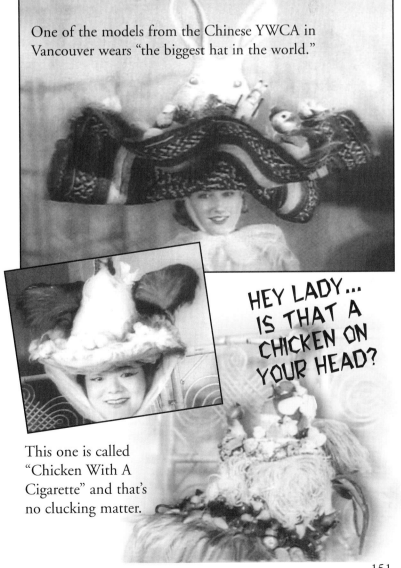

HEY LADY... IS THAT A CHICKEN ON YOUR HEAD?

This one is called "Chicken With A Cigarette" and that's no clucking matter.

Skyline
by Clarks

– fashion shoes
in a choice
of widths

Interleaf 79.9
Black suede or
Chinese white glacé
Fittings AA, B.

# BAINBRIDGE'S
MAURICE BAINBRIDGE LTD
Footwear Specialists

NOW IT'S
CRIPPS for Ladies' SHOES

OUR NEW SHOE DEPARTMENT IS OPEN

Van-Dal

Holmes

Hutchings

Ferragamo

I. Miller

Cripps

ERPOOL'S MOST FAMOUS FASHION HOUSE
VERYTHING IN LADIES FASHION VEAR

BOLD ST LIVERPOOL

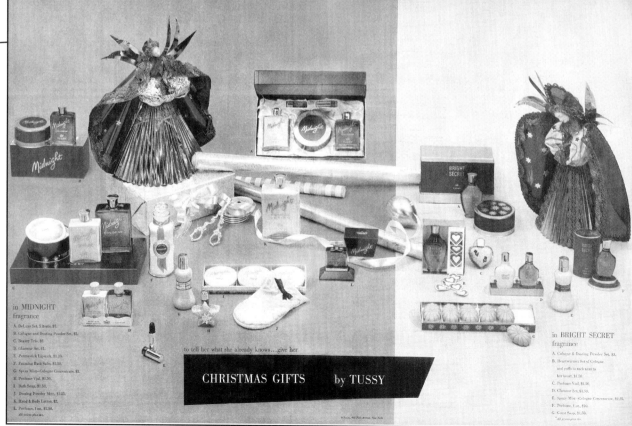

in MIDNIGHT
fragrance

to tell her what she already knows...give her

CHRISTMAS GIFTS    by TUSSY

in BRIGHT SECRET
fragrance

## Here's What The Experts Say About Wearing High Heels:

## TWO HEELS UP

- Physically and psychologically beneficial;
- High Heels throw the weight onto the heel instead of the toe;
- Eliminates slouching;
- Produces more healthy breathing;
- Adds inches to the bust;
- Men love long legs and heels give the impression of greater leg length.

## TWO HEELS DOWN

- Produces bow legs and knock knees and the Anti-Cruelty League would protest loudly if men tried to put animals into such a contraption.

# Shoes

Shoes are fancy with sharply pointed toes and range in fabrics from striped linen, flowered silk crepe and satin to velvet and lace.

Rosebud-printed leather with linen sides, high-rising tongue and buckled vamp, curved Louis heel. $17.95

Mottled silk-print pump with slim teardrop toe, bright jewel at center vamp. Mid-heel and collar are of blue kid. $14.95.

Smooth-calf pump with new low back, white underlay, tiny buckle on vamp. Needle-point heel is unbreakable. $19.95

Spectator calf teamed with gray kid, has high peaked throat-line and small tie at vamp. $12.95

Suede pump, with striped silk Edwardian tie, has the important needle toe, low back and Louis heel. $18.95

Ascot-gray calf pump with high pointed vamp, defined by white striping, has a curved Louis heel. $18.95

The longer, more tapering line in a pinpoint-toe flat. The soft white kid is set off by a gold Puritan buckle. $12.95

Saddle Shoes are in with the Levis' crowd and casual-wear fans. It doesn't hurt that Elvis Presley makes the scene in a pair of saddle shoes in *Jailhouse Rock.*

When people look at you (and they do)
90% of what
they see is your <u>clothes</u>!

Are <u>you</u> paying careful
attention to what you wear?
(other people are!)

# Dress Right - you

## How to
## Dress Right
### this spring

*Hooray, it's spring!*
Put pride in your stride.
Pay attention to your
clothes, and you'll feel
right because you'll *look*
right—in clothes that fit,
in colors that match, in
a hat that's up to date.
What you wear is as
much a part of the im-
pression you make as
your smile, your voice.
your handshake.

*Is there a secret* to dressing right? Not
really . . . it's a habit . . . a habit that pays
off in comfort and confidence. It begins with
noticing what looks well on others, it's dis-
covering what looks best on you. It's watch-
ing store windows, newspapers and magazines, keeping up with what's new, what's
flattering, what's fun. Most of all, it's paying attention to what you wear: the right
outfit for every occasion, the right style,
colors, accessories for you.

*Take stock now*—it's
spring-cleaning time!
Clear out those old, out-of-
date suits you never wear.
Replace worn-out shirts,
spotted ties, ragged shorts
and undershirts and faded
socks that don't stay up.

*Feel like a new man* this spring! A new
suit—a new pair of slacks and jacket—
can make you feel (and look) like a
million. (An *extra* suit can be a real
economy, because it lets you rotate your
clothes so that they actually last longer,
stay neater; they regain their shape
while they "rest" on a hanger.) How
about a lightweight formal jacket and
trousers for summer parties? You'll be
amazed how many new ideas there are
in this spring's crop. You can find the
best of them—in suits, shirts, slacks and
accessories galore—at the store near you
that displays the Dress Right symbol.

The way you look has much to do
with the <u>way</u> that people look at you!

# can't afford not to!

**American Institute
of Men's and Boys' Wear**

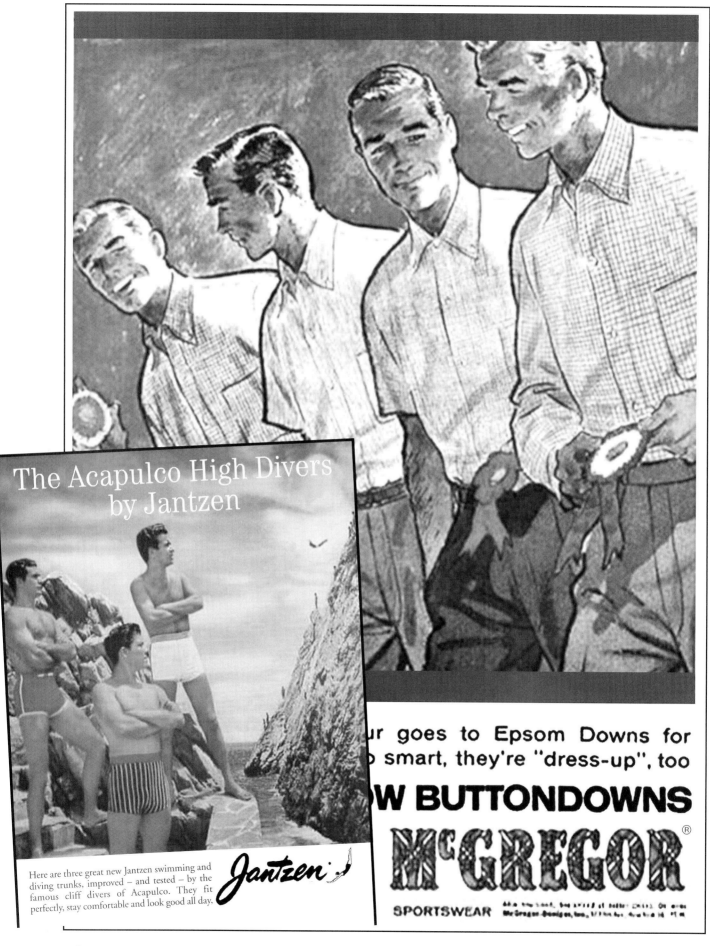

The Acapulco High Divers
by Jantzen

Here are three great new Jantzen swimming and diving trunks, improved – and tested – by the famous cliff divers of Acapulco. They fit perfectly, stay comfortable and look good all day,

*Jantzen*

ur goes to Epsom Downs for
smart, they're "dress-up", too

W BUTTONDOWNS

McGREGOR®

SPORTSWEAR

# MENSWEAR

Men are wearing suits made of man-made fibers: lightweight blends of Dacron and fine worsted. Small Glen Plaids seem to be a popular choice, while sports jackets are showing huge plaids and *4 buttons, not 6!* Other fashion moves are Hapi Coats made from Oriental silks and smoking or host jackets. Handkerchiefs are fashionable musts. A bit of fashion-daring is seen in scarves, ties and Ascots in paisley prints. Not to be outdone by the ladies, men take to fake furs!

Dark grey shadow-striped wool gabardine Ivy League slacks with leather trim on pockets. $7.95

**KANGOL**
**ONE PIECE**

**FLEXIBLE CAP**

Cotton velvet Host Coat with rayon trim on shawl collar, cuffs and pocket available in dark wine, navy and black. $35.00

Buick Super 4-Door Riviera

*When better automobiles are built Buick will build them*

# Roomiest hit in the Style Parade

**(Step in and s-t-r-e-t-c-h**

**—it's the Buick SUPER—and what a dream car to drive!)**

WE COULD give you facts and figures, chapter and verse, about the '57 Buick as the *roomiest* of America's best-selling cars.

And that's doubly true of the Buick SUPER pictured here.

Just step into a Buick SUPER—move your arms, relax your shoulders, cross your legs.

Then you'll know comfort that gets sweeter the longer you're there—and styling that looks smarter the longer you stare.

But that's only the start of the thrills you'll find in this most completely changed Buick in history. The real excitement comes from performance that makes this the dream car *to drive.*

**Power?** You have it, in abundance—for you boss more might than ever gave vigor to a Buick before.

**Response?** Like nothing in an earth-bound vehicle. For you have the instant action of today's new Dynaflow.*

**Ride? Handling? Roadability? Braking?** Try 'em and see!

Ask your Buick dealer for a demonstration—and for figures that make Buick your best buy today.

BUICK *Division of* GENERAL MOTORS

*\*New Advanced Variable Pitch Dynaflow is the only Dynaflow Buick builds today. It is standard on Roadmaster. Super and Century — optional at modest extra cost on the Special.*

**Only Buick brings you this built-in "conscience" SAFETY-BUZZER**

—a simple device that's a great boon to your safety. You merely preset the miles-per-hour you want. When you reach that pace, a warning buzzer sounds. Drop below that pace and the buzzer stops. Standard on ROADMASTER, optional at extra cost on other Series.

# Big Thrill's Buick

*SPECIAL · CENTURY · SUPER · ROADMASTER · and ROADMASTER 75*

Sports

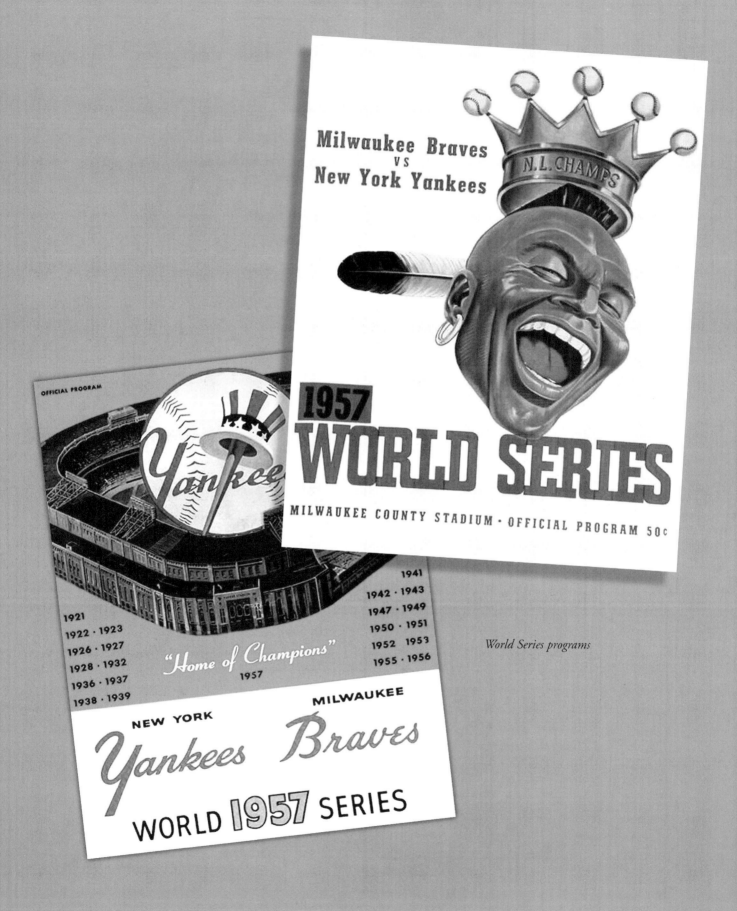

*World Series programs*

# SPORTS

## Braves Edge The Yankees 4-3, Winning The World Series

**Y**ankee slugger **Mickey Mantle** ("The Switcher") in the dugout with manager **Casey Stengel**.

**P**itcher **Lou Burdette** of the Braves pitches three victories, making Milwaukee the new champions and is named the World Series' Most Valuable Player.

FOR YOUR DRYNESS,

YOUR HIGHNESS...

THIS FRESH, CLEAN TASTE!

● Whatever level you operate at—a dry throat is a dry throat. And a fresh, clean taste is what you need for it.

Not just "something cold", mind you ... but 7-Up ... the sparkling drink that not only tastes fresh and cool going down, but leaves your mouth and throat cool when you *finish* the bottle. Results? No stickiness ... no come-back thirst ... just a real *cool you.*

*You like it...*
*it likes you!*

**Nothing does it like Seven-Up!**

# Baseball

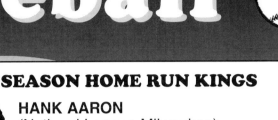

### SEASON HOME RUN KINGS

**HANK AARON**
(National League-Milwaukee)
44 Home Runs, 132 Runs Batted In
**ROY SIEVERS**
(American League-Washington)
42 Home Runs, 114 Runs Batted In

### CY YOUNG AWARD

**WARREN SPAHN**
Milwaukee

### NATIONAL LEAGUE BATTING CHAMPION

**STAN MUSIAL** (St. Louis Cardinals)
.351 Average

### AMERICAN LEAGUE BATTING CHAMPION

**TED WILLIAMS** (Boston Red Sox)
.388 Average

## MOST VALUABLE PLAYER

**AMERICAN LEAGUE**
**Mickey Mantle**
New York Yankees

**NATIONAL LEAGUE**
**Hank Aaron**
Milwaukee Braves

*Highest Paid Ball Player*
*TED WILLIAMS Signs $100,000 Contract With Boston Red Sox.*

## ROOKIE OF THE YEAR

**AMERICAN LEAGUE**
**Tony Kubek**
New York Yankees

**NATIONAL LEAGUE**
**Jack Sanford**
Philadelphia Phillies

"THE BUMS" **Brooklyn DODGERS**

GO WEST YOUNG MEN-- AND THEY WILL!
New York Loses Two of its Major League Ball Clubs to the West Coast—the Giants to San Francisco and the Brooklyn Dodgers to Los Angeles.

LOS ANGELES Dodgers

## JACKIE ROBINSON Announces He Will Retire From Baseball.

# 18,000 Enthusiastic Fans Jam Madison Square Garden To Watch The Contest Between Home Team CCNY And Oregon State.

CCNY scores the first points.

The Northwest team scores again in this close game, much to the chagrin of this CCNY fan.

Some of the players take a spill after Oregon blocks a CCNY attempt at scoring.

The home team boys finally wrap it up, winning 58-51.

*Wilt Chamberlain*

# BASKETBALL

## BOSTON CELTICS Beat ST. LOUIS HAWKS 4-3 For NBA Championship

•

### MOST VALUABLE PLAYER OF THE YEAR
### Bob Cousy (Boston Celtics)

### ROOKIE OF THE YEAR
### Tom Heinsohn (Boston Celtics)

### NUMBER 1 SCORER
### Paul Arizin 1,817 Points

•

## NORTH CAROLINA Edges KANSAS 54-53 For The NCAA Championship

•

### COLLEGE BOARDS

University Of Kansas' **Wilt ("The Stilt") Chamberlain** Is The Most Publicized College Basketball Player In A Generation.

With Several Years Of College Still Ahead Of Him, Seattle University's **Elgin Baylor** Is Deluged With Professional And Industrial-League Team Offers.

# ICE HOCKEY

• **Montreal Canadiens** Beat **Boston Bruins** 4-1 For Stanley Cup Win.

• **S**weden Wins The World And European Championships In Moscow. Protesting Soviet Repression Of Hungary, The U.S. And Canada Among Some Of The Nations Boycotting The Tournament.

*Question:*

## Why does Jack Kramer crave orange juice after a fast tennis match?

*Answer:*

## His Body Wisdom tells him he needs extra Vitamin C and quick energy!

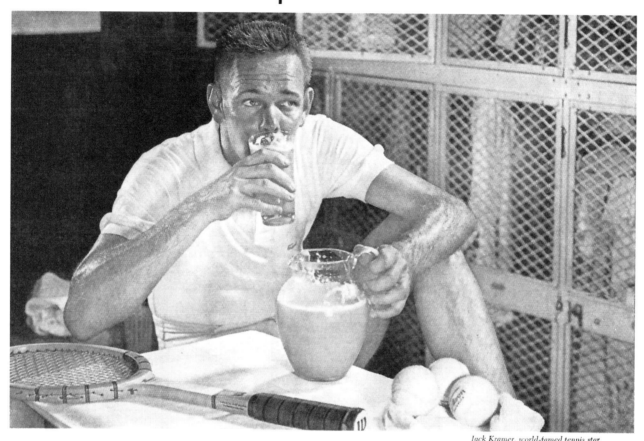

*Jack Kramer, world-famed tennis star*

## Are you active, busy?
## Then you need extra orange juice, too!

Stop and count—and you may find you cover as many miles per day as "Mr. Tennis" himself, and use up Vitamin C and energy just as fast. So when *you* have that same craving for a big, cool glass of orange juice, your Body Wisdom is telling you, too, to replenish Vitamin C and energy. You *need*

that extra juice, because—for busy, active people—having it with breakfast is just not enough.

Today, stock up on delicious Fresh-Frozen Orange Juice from Florida. It's rich in Vitamin C; it gives you quick energy. Make an *extra* pitcherful every morning!

*This little can makes 4 big glasses!*

Less than 5¢ a glass!

© Florida Citrus Commission, Lakeland, Florida, 1957

**CHILDREN** must have extra juice when they play hard to keep up energy and Vitamin C!

**OUTDOOR WORKERS** burn up Vitamin C and energy faster, must replace it often!

**MOTHERS-TO-BE** should double their intake of orange juice for extra Vitamin C!

## FRESH-FROZEN ORANGE JUICE *Packed with Florida Sunshine!*

# Althea Gibson First African-American To Win Wimbledon & U.S. Nationals

Althea Gibson is congratulated by Darlene Hard after Althea wins the Wimbledon championship.

Althea in action at Forest Hills, NY.

Queen Elizabeth herself presents the symbol of victory to this young woman from Harlem who is now the toast of the tennis world.

Sportsmen everywhere applaud her triumph and share in her moment of victory.

# TENNIS

## Australia Beats U.S. 3-2 To Win Davis Cup.

### U.S. Open Singles Championship

**Men:** **Malcolm Anderson** (over Ashley Cooper)
**Women:** **Althea Gibson** (over Louise Brough)

### Wimbledon

**Men:** **Lew Hoad** (over Ashley Cooper)
**Women:** **Althea Gibson** (over Darlene Hard)

# LOS ANGELES WOMAN WINS AAU DIVING MEET IN HOUSTON

**P**aula Jean Myers of Los Angeles sweeps all five diving meets.

**T**he beaming winner.

# NEW RECORDS IN TRACK & FIELD SET AT THE NCAA MEETS IN AUSTIN, TEXAS

George Bell, of Indiana, sets a new collegiate mark in the broad jump at 26´ 7˝.

George changes shoes after his fantastic jump.

# ICE SKATING

### WORLD FIGURE SKATING CHAMPIONSHIP

Men:      David Jenkins (U.S.)

Women:   Carol Heiss (U.S.)

### U.S. NATIONAL

Men:      David Jenkins

Women:   Carol Heiss

### CANADIAN NATIONAL

Men:      Charles Snelling

Women:   Carole Jane Pachl

# Believe It or Not!

**ENGINEERING B-W PRODUCTION** ™

**BORG-WARNER** SKILL AND INGENUITY BENEFIT ALMOST EVERY AMERICAN EVERY DAY THROUGH THE AUTOMOTIVE, AVIATION, MARINE, FARM MACHINERY AND HOME EQUIPMENT FIELDS!

19 OUT OF THE 20 MAKES OF CARS CONTAIN ESSENTIAL **B-W** PARTS. EVERY COMMERCIAL PLANE AND MANY SHIPS HAVE VITAL **B-W** COMPONENTS. 9 OUT OF 10 FARMS USE **B-W** EQUIPPED MACHINES. EVERY OIL FIELD USES **B-W** EQUIPMENT. MILLIONS OF HOMES HAVE **B-W** BUILDING MATERIALS, EQUIPMENT AND APPLIANCES.

SPRINKLERS OF B-W CYCOLAC "DISAPPEAR" WHEN NOT IN USE.

## AMERICANS STILL START 18 FOREST FIRES AN HOUR!

COOPERATION OF AMERICANS HAS HELPED REDUCE FOREST FIRE LOSSES BY TWO THIRDS DURING THE PAST DECADE. YET THE WOODLANDS BURNED LAST YEAR TOTALLED SOME 9,000,000 ACRES. CARELESSNESS ALONE STILL STARTS FOREST FIRES AT THE RATE OF ALMOST 500 A DAY! YOU CAN HELP CUT THIS WASTE JUST BY BEING CAREFUL WITH CIGARETTES AND MATCHES. **OBSERVE FORESTRY RULES!**

## THIRSTY ROOTS CAN NOW ORDER "RAIN" THEY NEED!

THE NEWEST LAWN SPRINKLING SYSTEM USES A BURIED MOISTURE "SENSER". WHENEVER ROOTS NEED WATER, IT TURNS ON SPRINKLERS THAT POP UP AND SPRAY. WHEN THE GROUND IS SOAKED, THE SYSTEM SHUTS ITSELF OFF. TO ASSURE DEPENDABLE OPERATION YEAR AFTER YEAR, VITAL PARTS, INCLUDING WATER LINES, FITTINGS, AND SPRINKLERS, ARE MADE OF CYCOLAC*. THIS TREMENDOUSLY TOUGH NEW PLASTIC FROM **B-W's MARBON CHEMICAL** WITHSTANDS GRIT, HEAT--EVEN WINTER FREEZING.

## JET PILOT HITS PLANES THAT ARE NEVER WHERE HE SEES THEM!

HUMAN EYES ARE TOO SLOW FOR JET-SPEED COMBAT. A PILOT SEES AN ENEMY JET CUTTING IN FRONT OF HIM ONLY AS A PHANTOM-- AN AFTER-IMAGE. ACTUALLY IT IS 88 FEET OR MORE BEYOND. BUT THE NEWEST FIRE-CONTROL SYSTEM "SEES" THE REAL TARGET. IT THEN FLIES HIS PLANE ON A DEAD AIM COURSE BY MEANS OF SENSITIVE CONTROL MECHANISMS FROM **B-W's WESTON HYDRAULICS.** RESPONDING WITH SPLIT-SECOND SPEED TO A STREAM OF ELECTRICAL SIGNALS, THESE MECHANISMS "STEER" THE PLANE UNERRINGLY TO ASSURE A DIRECT HIT WHEN THE WEAPONS FIRE.

*Jim Brown*

**Supreme Court Places Pro Football Under Anti-Trust Laws**

**Former Syracuse Star, JIM BROWN, Debuts With The Cleveland Browns**

# FOOTBALL

## DETROIT LIONS Beat CLEVELAND BROWNS 59-14
### For The NFL Championship

## IOWA Trounces OREGON STATE 35-19
### Winning Rose Bowl Competition

## NOTRE DAME Beats OKLAHOMA 7-0 Breaking
### Oklahoma's Four-Year Winning Streak

## JIM THORPE TROPHY WINNER
### Johnny Unitas, Baltimore Colts

**CANADIAN FOOTBALL LEAGUE CHAMPION (GREY CUP)**

**Hamilton Tiger-Cats Beat Winnipeg Blue Bombers 32-7**

**John Crow**, Texas A&M's All-American halfback is this year's winner of the Heisman Trophy.

"SUGAR" RAY ROBINSON Defeats GENE FULLMER, Regaining Middleweight Title For The Fourth Time.

•

CARMEN BASILIO Defeats "SUGAR" RAY ROBINSON, Winning The Middleweight Boxing Championship.

•

FLOYD PATTERSON Beats TOMMY JACKSON In New York Bout Retaining Heavyweight Title.

•

ARCHIE MOORE Retains His Light Heavyweight Title Knocking Out Tony Anthony In The Seventh Round.

•

Six New Members Are Elected Into The Boxing Hall Of Fame: CHARLEY MITCHELL, KID MCCOY, PACKY MCFARLAND, LES DARCY, BATTLING NELSON And JOHNNY DUNDEE.

# BOXING

# AUTO RACING

**INDIANAPOLIS 500 WINNER**
Sam Hanks (135.601 MPH)

•

**WORLD PRIX GRAND CHAMPION**
Juan Fangio, Argentina

# CYCLING

**TOUR DE FRANCE WINNER**
Jacques Anquetil (France)

•

**UNITED STATES CHAMPION**
Jack Disney

•

**WORLD CHAMPION**
Rik van Steenbergen (Belgium)

# RACING

 **THE WINNERS**

KENTUCKY DERBY
  "Iron Liege"- Bill Hartack, Jockey
PREAKNESS
  "Bold Ruler"- Eddie Arcaro, Jockey
BELMONT STAKES
  "Gallant Man"- Willie Shoemaker, Jockey

**The First National Wheelchair Games Are Held At Adelphi College In Garden City, New York Including Table Tennis, Javelin And The 60-Yard Dash.**

## SWIMMING

Danish Olympic Swimming Champion **GRETA ANDERSEN** Wins Coed Race Across The English Channel Covering The Distance In 13 Hours And 53 Minutes.

**Bill Munsey** wins the Speedboat Gold Cup Race on Lake Washington in Seattle.

# U.S. OLYMPIC WINNER BRINGS HOME A BRIDE

After weeks of pleading, American Olympic winner HAROLD CONNOLLY gets approval from the Czech government to allow him to bring his bride, Olympic winner OLGA FIKOTOVA, to the United States. They only have $.35 between them but look forward to a rosy future.

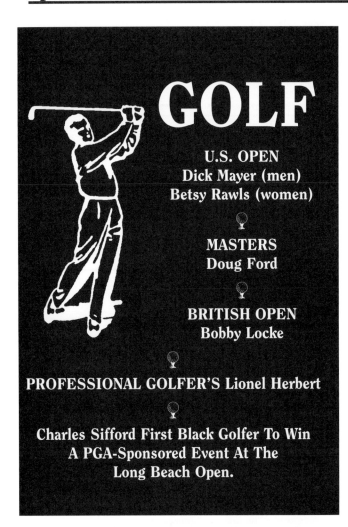

# GOLF

**U.S. OPEN**
Dick Mayer (men)
Betsy Rawls (women)

**MASTERS**
Doug Ford

**BRITISH OPEN**
Bobby Locke

**PROFESSIONAL GOLFER'S** Lionel Herbert

**Charles Sifford First Black Golfer To Win A PGA-Sponsored Event At The Long Beach Open.**

# CHESS

**14-Year Old BOBBY FISCHER Becomes Open Champion Of U.S. Chess Federation.**

**VASSILY SMYSLOV Dethrones MIKHAIL BOTVINNIK'S 9-Year Reign As World Chess Champion.**

# BILLIARDS

**World 3-Cushion Champion**
Harold Worst, Chicago, Ill.

**U.S. Open 3-Cushion Champion**
Arthur Rubin, Brooklyn, NY

**U.S. Pocket Billiards**
Luther Lassiter, Elizabeth City, N.C.

**World Pocket Crown**
Willie Mosconi, Philadelphia, Pa.

# BOWLING

**54TH American Bowling Congress Champion**
Jim Spalding, Louisville, KY.
Record Score: 2,088

Born in 1957
Evelyn Ashford

# TRACK & FIELD

London's White City Stadium Is The Site Of The Greatest Mile Race Of All Time When Four Runners In The Same Event Run The Distance In Less Than 4 Minutes.

University Of Pennsylvania Track Star Bruce Dern Resigns From Team Rather Than Shave His Sideburns.

**The International Olympic Committee Votes To Add Volleyball And Archery To Its Sports Line-Up.**

**FLICKBACK** has the perfect gift to bring a nostalgic smile to the lips of anyone celebrating a birthday, anniversary or reunion. Or, why not treat yourself?

*Your friend or loved one will be delighted to receive the original* **FLICKBACK**, *the colorful DVD Gift Card full of stories and pictures from their fabulous year. The collector's DVD presents entertaining highlights featuring the people and events that made their year special. A dedication page conveys your personal message and an envelope is included for mailing.*

**WHAT A YEAR IT WAS!** *is a lavish, 176-page hardcover "scrapbook" packed with stories, photos and artwork detailing the movies, music, shows, sports, fashion, news, people, places and events that make a year unique and memorable. A special dedication page completes a truly personal yearbook gift which will be treasured for years to come.*

Products are available for years 1929 through 1979.

Video products are also available in VHS format.

Explore our website or call to find a **FLICKBACK** retailer near you.

www. FLICKBACK .com

(800) 541-3533